The Five Biggest Ideas in Science

Charles M. Wynn
and
Arthur W. Wiggins

D0179204

With Cartoon Commentary
by Sidney Harris

John Wiley & Sons, Inc.
New York • Chichester • Brisbane • Toronto
Singapore • Weinheim

Published by John Wiley & Sons, Inc.

The cartoons on pages iv, 11, 25, 34, 41, 51, 57, 58, 61, 63, 66, 72, 74, 82, 85, 108, 116, 133, and 134 first appeared in *American Scientist* © 1988, 1981, 1987, 1981, 1977, 1981, 1984, 1981, 1975, 1980, 1984, 1977, 1989, 1981, 1986, 1978, 1976, 1983, and 1976, respectively.

The cartoon on page 1 first appeared in *Today's Chemist* © 1990.

The cartoons on pages 9, 49, 52, and 98 first appeared in *Science* © 1980, 1982, 1980, and 1990, respectively.

The cartoon on page 15 first appeared in *Clinical Chemistry News* © 1980.

The cartoon on page 62 first appeared in *Physics Today* © 1991.

The cartoon on page 76 first appeared in the *New York Times* © 1982.

The cartoon on page 121 first appeared in *Fantasy and Science Fiction* © 1991.

Library of Congress Cataloging-in-Publication Data

Wynn, Charles M.
     The five biggest ideas in science / Charles M. Wynn and Arthur W.
Wiggins ; with cartoon commentary by Sidney Harris.
          p.   cm.
     Includes bibliographical references and index.
     Summary: Presents five basic scientific hypotheses: the atomic
model, the periodic law, the big bang theory, plate tectonics, and
evolution.
     ISBN 0-471-13812-6 (pbk. : alk. paper)
     1. Science—Miscellanea.   [1. Science—Miscellanea.]
I. Wiggins, Arthur W.   II. Harris, Sidney, ill.   III. Title.
Q163.W99   1997
500—dc20   96-27469
                                                                   CIP
                                                                    AC

Printed in the United States of America

10 9 8 7 6 5 4 3 2 1

Contents

	Prologue	v
1	The Road to Discovery: The Method of Science	1
2	BIG IDEA #1 Physics' Model of the Atom: Seeing the Unseeable	13
3	BIG IDEA #2 Chemistry's Periodic Law: Sorting the Elements	31
4	BIG IDEA #3 Astronomy's Big Bang Theory: Tracing the Elements' Roots	47
5	BIG IDEA #4 Geology's Plate Tectonics Model: Down to Earth	65
6	BIG IDEA #5 Biology's Theory of Evolution: Life Begins and Branches Out	81
7	The Method of Science: Further Insights	107
8	Benefit/Risk Analysis: Potential Applications of Scientific Knowledge	119
	Epilogue	139
	Idea Folders	143
	Additional Reading	185
	Index	189

Prologue

Can just five fundamental ideas open up a way to comprehend, appreciate, and evaluate the world of science? Taken as a group, the five ideas in this book do exactly that. Chosen especially for their power to explain phenomena, they provide a comprehensive survey of science.

Each idea represents science's tentative answer to a question about natural and artificial phenomena. We say "tentative" because, as you will see, science is a *never-ending* search for answers to the universe's mysteries. This book takes away some of the mystery and invites you to discover the reasoning that is the essence of science itself.

Beginning with a search for the basic building blocks in the universe (essentially, atoms), we will explore the behavior of the different kinds of atoms that make up the universe. We'll go on to ponder the past, present, and future states of the universe, consider the nature of our home planet, and, finally, study life on Earth from a molecular perspective. Here, then, is our list of the five biggest ideas and the questions that they answer.

Question   Do basic building blocks of matter exist? If so, what do they look like?

Answer   BIG IDEA #1—Physics' Model of the Atom

Question   What relationships, if any, exist among different kinds of atoms, the basic building blocks of the universe?

Answer   BIG IDEA #2—Chemistry's Periodic Law

Question   Where did the atoms of the universe come from, and what is their destiny?

Answer   BIG IDEA #3—Astronomy's Big Bang Theory

Question   How is the matter of the universe arranged in planet Earth?

Answer   BIG IDEA #4—Geology's Plate Tectonics Model

Question   How did life on Earth originate and develop?

Answer   BIG IDEA #5—Biology's Theory of Evolution

These and other scientific ideas are just ideas until someone makes decisions about whether and how to apply them and weighs the potential benefits of a proposed action against potential risks. We'll show you how to use benefit/risk analysis to evaluate potential applications of scientific

"BUT THIS IS THE SIMPLIFIED VERSION FOR THE GENERAL PUBLIC."

ideas and to unlock their potential power to produce changes.

Finally, you'll discover a collection of Idea Folders on a wide variety of topics related to the five biggest ideas. Idea folders relevant to each chapter are listed at the end of the chapter.

Sidney Harris, America's foremost science cartoonist, has provided cartoon commentary to punctuate our prose and illuminate its meanings. His humor, like all humor, arises from the unexpected and the incongruous. It surprises us into a new point of view. Appreciation of Sidney's humor requires sufficient background and insight in order to recognize something as unexpected or incongruous. We provide the background and insight—you get the joke.

Enjoy!

Willimantic, Connecticut   C.M.W.
Bloomfield Hills, Michigan   A.W.W.
New Haven, Connecticut   S.H.

CHAPTER ONE

The Road to Discovery

The Method of Science

K-9 Hypothesis

Thinking like a scientist does not require incredibly precise, highly sophisticated, other-worldly logic. Consider this homely example:

A few months ago you bought a puppy named Domino. You have gotten to know him pretty well during these months. You have been observing his behavior under all weather conditions. Domino prefers to stay outside most of the time. But, shortly before a storm, you have noticed that he begins barking—he wants to come inside. By now you have come to react to that kind of barking by first closing the windows and then bringing him inside. He's got you trained! One day he starts barking. You presume a storm is coming and close the windows; but, when you go outside to untie him, you are surprised to find that the sky is clear and the wind is quite gentle. You note that a bigger dog is skulking away now that you have arrived on the scene. From now on, you will be aware that Domino's "prestorm" barking is an alarm system, generally predicting a storm and occasionally signaling the defense of his territory.

Your approach to making sense out of Domino's world is similar to that used by all scientists. At first you were involved in *observation,* somehow sensing (seeing, hearing, feeling, tasting, or feeling) a pattern in events: Domino barks in a particular way at certain times.

Next, you formed a *hypothesis,* creating a general statement about the basic nature of the phenomenon observed: Whenever Domino barks that way, storms occur.

Then you made a *prediction,* applying your hypothesis to a subsequent situation: Domino is barking in his prestorm way, so it will soon rain.

Finally, you performed an *experiment,* or test of the prediction, by looking for an actual occurrence of the phenomenon predicted to determine whether the prediction was true or false. Because an experiment yielded results (no postbarking rain) that differed from the prediction, the hypothesis had to be revised, or modified to explain the experiment results. Then you *recycled* through the procedure, using the revised hypothesis (see Figure 1-1).

K-9 Theories and Laws

Once the hypothesis is modified—Domino barks when he is alarmed by something that frightens him—new predictions can be made and new experiments done to check out the predictions. Each time a prediction is supported by an experiment, the hypothesis gains credibility and dependability. After many successful tests of the hypothesis, it might be called a *theory* (in this case, another "Domino Theory"). Theories frequently explain a *law*, which is a statement of some kind of regularity in nature. Theories might postulate the underlying cause(s) of a law's regularity, as when a law about the frequency of Domino's barking and the frequency of rain is explained by a theory that he barks because he is frightened.

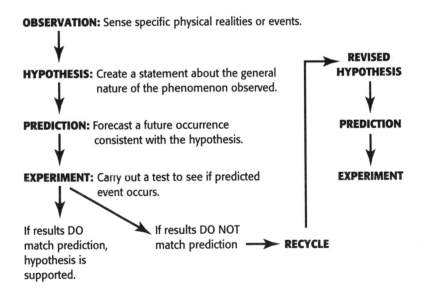

OBSERVATION: Sense specific physical realities or events.

HYPOTHESIS: Create a statement about the general nature of the phenomenon observed.

PREDICTION: Forecast a future occurrence consistent with the hypothesis.

EXPERIMENT: Carry out a test to see if predicted event occurs.

If results DO match prediction, hypothesis is supported.

If results DO NOT match prediction ➝ **RECYCLE**

REVISED HYPOTHESIS

PREDICTION

EXPERIMENT

FIGURE 1-1. The Method of Science

Of course, some day, that kind of barking might result from a splinter off Domino's dog house! A slight modification of the hypothesis can accommodate this new finding.

So what conclusions can be drawn from the K-9 inquiry?

It Seems as If . . .

You observe things all the time. You make special notice of certain of those observations because they seem to fit together in some way. That apparent pattern, explanation, or relationship is a hypothesis about the phenomenon under consideration. The hypothesis is tentative by its very nature: *It seems as if* whenever Domino barks that way, storms occur.

I'll Bet That . . .

While the hypothesis might seem plausible at the time, it must be put to the test by making a prediction about a future event. The prediction is a kind of bet that this future event will correspond with the hypothesis: *I'll bet that* the next time Domino barks like that, it will soon rain. If this bet is won, the payoff is added credibility to the hypothesis. There's even a payoff if the bet is lost: increased insight into the workings of the universe.

To make and test a prediction is to take a risk, namely that the hypothesis will be shown to be in error. However, if you do not make and test predictions, you risk believing in incorrect ideas. For science to grow, it must take risks; prediction is the risk that keeps science growing.

It is important to remember that the predictions that are borne out *do not* (cannot!) prove that a hypothesis is correct. They simply provide additional support for belief in the hypothesis. Remember that splinter on Domino's dog house!

This general sequence, as shown in Figure 1-1, is what is referred to as the method of science, or *scientific method*.

Is There Really a Method?

Some people argue that there is no such thing as one, singular method of science. They argue that discussions such as this make it appear that one could simply apply these steps in sequence to make discoveries and to solve any scientific problem. Undoubtedly, the actual work of the scientist is much less formal. It is not always done in a clearly logical and systematic way. It involves intellectual inventiveness, the creation of mental images of what has never been actually experienced, and even the devising and testing of strong intuitive feelings.

So please do not get the idea that this scientific method is some kind of automatic procedure. Although proponents of artificial intelligence have hopes of developing a machine that can program the selection of appropriate observations or the imaginative act involved in the formation of a hypothesis, others contend that there is something in the activity of the brain that transcends that of any machine.

Some would argue that science begins not with observations or "facts," but with problems. It is true that sometimes a scientist might not have noted a fact had he or she not been thinking about a certain problem. By contrast, a single observation or fact might be so unusual as to force itself upon the viewer and, in the process, *create* a problem. Furthermore, what is observed depends not only upon what there is to be seen, but also upon what the viewer has seen before.

Although there is merit in these points of view, the method of science will nevertheless be used throughout this book to rationally reconstruct progress in science. Although big, scientific discoveries are rarely, if ever, made by applying a series of logical rules to known facts, it is always possible *after* a discovery to construct a logical path to it.

For instance, Dr. Robin Cook, author of the bestseller *Coma*, claims that using the scientific method led to his first successful book and film. Cook says he "went about the whole thing—hardcover, paperback, movie—in a planning sort of way." He decided to write a book that would appeal to as wide an audience as possible. He *observed* ten years of the *New York Times* best sellers list and studied it, finally deciding that mystery-thrillers seemed to have the best sales record. Then he started reading books, 200 in all. He sifted and analyzed, took many notes, and eventually arrived at a *hypothesis* about the ingredients for a best seller. Cook methodically applied his formula, as he *predicted* that the ingredients he was weaving into *Coma* would result in a best seller. His *experiment* was a multi-million-dollar success!

Models and Black Boxes

A hypothesis can take the form of a *model,* which is a representation or likeness of reality invented to account for observed phenomena. Model airplanes, model railroads, model cars, or model boats are all examples of physical models, similar to the real thing but different in size, material, complexity, and so on. Note that physical models might differ in the degree to which they simulate the actual object. A PT boat might be represented by a peanut shell floating down a stream or by a radio-controlled scale model.

Very often, models are formulated for objects whose contents cannot be observed. For example, take the question of whether a woman will give birth to a single child or twins. Before ultrasound photography was available, one could poke around, listen for two separate heartbeats, and create a model or image of what is inside. One of the authors faced this very situation when, even at the last minute, the doctors and nurses were making bets about his own child (children). (It was *a* boy!)

Something that is hidden from view is said to be "inside a black box." Birthday gifts are good examples of black boxes. Before being unwrapped, they are shaken, squeezed, and weighed to help formulate hypotheses about their contents. "It feels like a baseball. It rolls around like a baseball. It has the heft of a baseball. Oh no, it is a cheese ball!"

The Professor and the Midget

Here is another example of alternative hypotheses about the contents of a black box. Most people have dealt with the devilish instrument known as the automatic coffee vending machine. The reason for the expletives people use when talking about them is that the darn things do not always do as they are told. You put in three quarters for a 65¢ coffee. Sometimes, all goes well: The coins drop; amidst gearlike noises, your dime change emerges at about the same time as the cup falls; a gushing sound is heard; and your coffee, with the desired extra cream and extra sugar, fills the cup nearly to the top. Other days, however, it seems as if the machine has a mind of its own: The machine eats your quarters and goes silent; or, you get soup; or, you get two dimes back instead of one (this seldom happens).

The generally accepted hypothesis about the nature of coffee machines is: A series of gears, pipes, and gadgets are arranged so that certain coins will activate a process in which a cup is dispensed and filled. Unless you actually open such a machine, you can only make a hypothesis about its contents; so, in this sense, it is a black box.

Consider the following academic attempt to get to the bottom of this mystery.

Professor	*My* model for the automatic coffee vending machine that you have described is that a midget lives inside. Somehow the coins activate *him.* Remember this machine is a black box, so no peeking inside.
Student	Well, that's silly. Nobody is going to accept that hypothesis. A midget would starve after a while.
Professor	Well, when he gets too hungry, his performance is not up to par, as you have observed. The company has seen to it, however, that he is supplied with space food and all the coffee he can drink!
Student	I will pull out the plug and see if the machine still works. A midget should be able to work the mechanisms himself.
Professor	It is dark in there without electric lights—so, no electricity, no coffee. But my hypothesis is still all right.
Student	This will sound bizarre, but you started it. I could inject tear gas into the coin slot. The midget would cough.
Professor	He is equipped with a gas mask.
Student	I would play awful music until he screamed for relief.
Professor	He is deaf.

One could go on and on with this. Can you convince the professor to change her hypothesis? Go ahead and try. Notice that the professor did have to make a number of modifications of her original hypothesis. You see this refining of hypotheses again and again during the discussion of each of the big ideas.

At this point, you have no definitive experimental evidence to help you decide whether the purely mechanical model or the mechanical model operated by a deaf, space-food-eating, gas-mask-equipped midget is more appropriate.

Occam's Closer Shave

In cases such as the coffee machine, an additional test applied to the hypotheses is a test of economy or simplicity called *Occam's Razor,* named after William of Occam, an English philosopher. The test says that *the accepted hypothesis should be the simplest hypothesis that explains any given phenomenon.* Complexity might indeed be justified, but only with appropriate experimental evidence. Applying this test to the coffee machine, you find that the deaf, space-food-eating, gas-mask-equipped midget is just too complicated.

Recognizing the limitations of the method of science and the tendency toward simplification expressed in Occam's Razor, one might expect scientific works to be fragile and tentative, perhaps even oversimplified. Indeed, a total understanding of the workings of the whole universe remains an elusive goal of science. Yet, the partial understanding thus far achieved has fostered the development of technology that has drastically altered culture on Earth and reshaped its surface over the last several hundred years.

EINSTEIN SIMPLIFIED

Science's Domains

In this book, you will be examining what are considered to be the most important hypotheses generated in the sciences. Before proceeding, however, you should gain a sense of perspective about the various domains of science through an examination of the range of sizes of the entities studied by scientists.

The world with which you are most familiar is the world that you perceive with your senses—the world you can manipulate, hear, smell, taste, see, and feel. To aid or augment your senses, you can use various instruments to help make observations about portions of this world. For example, ordinary microscopes make it possible to view extremely small items. There is, however, a limit to the size of an item you can see with ordinary microscopes. Electron microscopes make it possible to see even smaller items; but electron microscopes do not use visible light, and, hence, you do not "see" in the usual sense. Beyond these limits lies the world of the extremely small: individual atoms and subatomic particles. If such objects cannot be seen, you might wonder (1) how their existence can be known and (2) how anything can be known about their nature? How can people believe in something they cannot hope to see?

And yet, they do believe. It is the same kind of belief as believing in the inner workings of an automatic coffee machine or in an unopened birthday present. The atom is a kind of black box whose interior can be described with the aid of some ingenious observations, as will be seen shortly.

At the other end of the scale, there is a domain whose magnitude is so immense that it cannot be easily comprehended—it cannot be sensed directly. It is so big or so far away that the capacity to make observations of it or to perform experiments on it is severely limited. Other planets, solar systems, stars, black holes, and galaxies inhabit this vast universe. If no one can get close enough to make detailed observations or to perform the desired experiments, how can acceptable hypotheses be formulated? With great tentativeness!

The belief in specific models of the solar system, stars, galaxies, and the universe itself is based on observations made by using powerful telescopes and other instruments that extend human senses, by sending out space probes, and by other methods. Hypotheses consistent with whatever is observed are then created. More than one hypothesis can be consistent with the observations. As further information becomes available, one particular hypothesis might be chosen or a new hypothesis formulated.

So, although there is only one universe that can be studied (could there be others?), it can be explored from the tiny world of atoms to the vastness of the universe itself.

To get a sense of perspective about the disciplines that study the five biggest ideas, you should note that:

- Astronomy deals essentially with the entirety of the universe.
- Physics deals with everything from the world of subatomic particles to the functioning of stars and galaxies.
- Chemistry deals with atoms and their interactions, but these are found all over the cosmos.
- Geology, probably more than any of the other sciences, draws from the other disciplines, utilizing direct sensing as well as probing beyond the limits of the senses.
- Biology studies life wherever it is found, as it exists on this planet and as it possibly exists elsewhere.

Idea Folders

1 Philosophical Presuppositions of Science

2 Serendipity and Progress in Science

3 Occam's Razor at Work: Space Travelers from the Past

4 Big and Small Things

CHAPTER TWO

Big Idea #1

Physics' Model of the Atom: Seeing the Unseeable

The universe is full of magical things,
patiently waiting for our wits to grow
sharper.

Eden Phillpotts

This study of science will begin in the realm of the very small. Suppose you were cooking a stew, and the recipe called for you to dice some carrots. You might get carried away and dice them so small that your knife could not cut them any more. The question might then occur to you: Is there any limit to this subdividing process, or could this subdividing, at least in principle, go on indefinitely? This is not a new question.

Aristotle versus Democritus

Aristotle (384–322 B.C.), a Greek philosopher, deduced the nature of things from a set of principles that to him were "self-evident." His hypothesis was that matter was continuous—it could be subdivided indefinitely, without ever reaching any limit. His basic position was that there is no ultimate underlying structure to matter.

Another Greek philosopher, Democritus (about 460–370 B.C.), is said to have reasoned as follows: While walking along a beach, he wondered whether the water in the sea was continuous or not. He knew that from a distance sand appeared continuous, but close up, sand was actually tiny grains. Similarly, he imagined that water could be divided into smaller and smaller drops and ultimately into "grains" of water. He, therefore, took the view that matter was discontinuous, that there was some point beyond which matter could no longer be subdivided.

Thus, according to Democritus, there is an ultimate underlying structure to matter. He called this smallest unit of matter the *atom* (from the Greek *a tomos*—"not cuttable"), a basic unit that he felt was indivisible (indestructible). Not only did Democritus's hypothesis postulate the existence of atoms, it also postulated the shapes of atoms. He imagined that atoms of water might be round balls and that atoms of fire could have sharp edges. The simplest (most symmetrical) of his atomic shapes was the spherical one shown in Figure 2-1, and it is that model that will be considered first.

Settling Scientific Disagreements

On what basis could this disagreement on continuity be resolved? In the time of Aristotle and Democritus, experi-

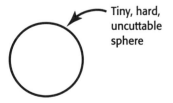

Tiny, hard, uncuttable sphere

FIGURE 2-1. Democritus's Model of the Atom

"WHAT I ESPECIALLY LIKE ABOUT BEING A
PHILOSOPHER-SCIENTIST IS THAT I DON'T HAVE TO
GET MY HANDS DIRTY."

mentation was *not* used in any systematic way to decide between alternative hypotheses. Observations led to hypotheses, but the process, in general, ended right there. Greek philosophers distrusted or were indifferent to experiments. They preferred to develop ideas by reason alone.

As a result, the acceptability of a hypothesis had to be based upon the *authority* of a philosopher. The hypothesis of the philosopher with the most persuasive power had the greatest acceptance. Aristotle was considered the greater authority, and thus his hypothesis was considered superior to that of Democritus.

For almost the next 2,000 years, science continued to be under the control of the authorities, who made few changes in the overall approach to science. Finally, the mood of the people began to shift toward more independence, and the works of Aristotle and Democritus were reexamined. By the 1500s and 1600s, learned societies and academies had arisen that paved the way for a revolutionary change in how science was done. The philosophical basis for this scientific revolution was expressed in the writings of Francis Bacon and others, who urged that no principles be taken as self-evident and that EXPERIMENTATION become the test of the credibility of a hypothesis.

Dalton's Billiard Balls

This testing approach was used by John Dalton, an English chemist, who, in 1803, was able to provide experimental evidence for Democritus's belief in atoms. He *observed* that substances, known as *compounds,* that consist of two or more simpler substances, known as *elements,* always contain these elements in the same proportions by mass—their composition by mass is constant. This relationship is known as the *Law of Constant Composition.*

Recall that laws are frequently explained by theories. To explain the Law of Constant Composition, Dalton resurrected Democritus's concept and said that elements are composed of extremely small, indestructible, indivisible particles called atoms. Dalton pictured these atoms as miniature billiard balls.

Dalton further theorized that an atom of a given element has its own fixed mass. Dalton's theory about atoms enabled him to offer an explanation for the relationship among the masses of the elements in a compound. He reasoned that if a compound is characterized by a fixed mass ratio of its component elements and if each atom of a given element has the same mass, then their proportion by mass—the compound's composition—must always be constant. (If the size of each combining unit was variable, the proportion by mass in compounds would also be variable, that is, not constant.)

It took about 2,000 years for scientists to accept *an* atomic model of matter. Dalton's model, however, is not the model conceptualized by today's scientists, for atoms are far more complex than billiard balls.

Thomson's Plum Pudding

Evidence for a more detailed atomic structure was provided in 1898 by Joseph John Thomson, an English physicist working at the famous Cavendish Laboratory at Cambridge University. Using gas discharge tubes (glass tubes with most of the air pumped out and with electrodes at either end), Thomson made a number of *observations*. He was trying to understand the nature of the strange glowing ray that was emitted within the tube when the electric current was turned on. These rays were called *cathode rays* because they came from the negative terminal called a cathode.

Thomson noted that the ray was attracted by a positively charged plate and repelled by a negatively charged one. He thereby deduced that the ray carried a negative charge. (Unlike charges attract; like charges repel.) He calculated the mass of these moving, negatively charged particles (now called *electrons*) to be about 2,000 times smaller than the mass of the lightest known atom, the hydrogen atom. Thus, they were constituents of atoms, and not simply charged atoms. Because electrons were emitted from electrodes made of a wide variety of materials, he was able to conclude that *all* of these substances must contain electrons.

Thomson had concluded that there *are* small subdivisions of matter. This supports Democritus's notion of matter being discontinuous and argues against Aristotle's notion of matter being continuous. In Aristotle's model, subdivisions of matter would just yield smaller and smaller pieces of the same material, but never a simple entity like the electron. Thomson also concluded that atoms are *not* indivisible, as Democritus had suggested. Atoms have subdivisions, namely, electrons. Atoms of gold are different from atoms of silver, but both contain electrons.

Thomson reasoned further that if matter in general is not electrically charged and yet electrons are *negatively* charged, then there must be *positively* charged material somewhere within the atom to counterbalance the electron's negativeness. Thomson did not know exactly where

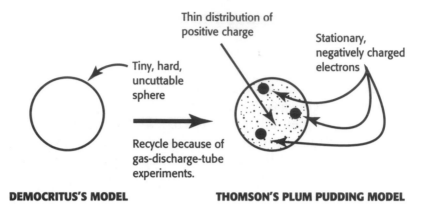

FIGURE 2-2. Democritus's and Thomson's Atom Models

this positive charge was located, but he decided to take a stab and formulate his *hypothesis,* which became known as the *Thomson Plum Pudding Model of the Atom:* An atom is spherical in shape and consists of a thin cloud of positively charged material, with some negatively charged particles called electrons sprinkled throughout, like raisins in plum pudding, as shown in Figure 2-2.

Note that Thomson's model of the atom kept one feature of Democritus's model, the spherical shape. Because there was no experimental evidence to the contrary, the principle of simplicity known as Occam's Razor held forth. A sphere, the most symmetric, solid geometric shape, was retained.

Rutherford's Solar System

To test Thomson's Plum Pudding Model, some prediction based upon the model had to be evaluated experimentally. To accomplish this, an experimental probe capable of penetrating the atom was needed. Then a prediction could be made of what effects that probe should have, and an experiment could be performed to find out what actually happens. This was no easy job because atoms are so tiny that it was difficult to find a small enough probe.

Another discovery of the time (around 1900) came to the rescue: radioactivity. It was found that some minerals gave off several kinds of rays spontaneously. One of the rays given off by these radioactive materials was positively charged. It was composed of positively charged particles called *alpha particles*. Thomson's successor at the Cavendish Laboratories, Lord Ernest Rutherford, decided to use these subatomic "bullets" to try to penetrate the gold atoms in a thin, gold foil target. Using the Thomson Plum Pudding Model of the Atom, Rutherford *predicted* (around 1911) that the alpha particles, which are about 7,400 times heavier than electrons, would rip right through Thomson's more-or-less-evenly-spread-out, much-less-compact pudding and light up a screen (similar to a TV screen) on the other side. He and his assistants set up the apparatus and did the *experiment*.

Sure enough, most of the alpha particles ripped right through, but an unexpectedly large number were deflected greatly, and a few even bounced back—they were reflected! Rutherford remarked, "It was quite the most incredible thing that ever happened to me in my life. It was almost like firing a 15-inch shell at some tissue paper and having it bounce back." Rutherford's predictions and experiment are shown in Figure 2-3.

Experiments that yield unexpected results do not upset the scientific applecart for long. Scientists *recycle* the hypothesis. Much as it must have bothered Rutherford to have to correct his predecessor, he was compelled to formulate a new hypothesis. What kind of model is consistent with Rutherford's experimental results?

Rutherford explained these results in his *Solar System Model of the Atom*. In this model, the atom is still depicted as spherical in shape. It consists of a relatively tiny central nucleus containing all of the positive charge and most of the mass, with electrons being distributed throughout most of the space occupied by the atom and orbiting the nucleus (the way the planets orbit the sun). Rutherford believed the electrons must be moving rapidly around outside this nucleus: If they were not moving, the electrical attraction of the positively

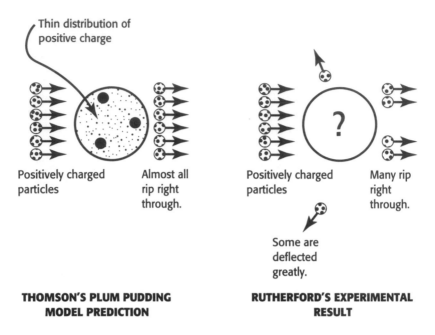

FIGURE 2-3. Predicted and Actual Result of Rutherford's Experiment

charged nucleus for the negatively charged electrons would cause the electrons to spiral into the nucleus, and the atom would collapse! Because most of the space in his model was occupied by the relatively flimsy electrons, most of the particles shot at the atoms would be expected to miss the tiny nucleus entirely and pass right through. Those few particles that happened to brush close to the nucleus or hit it head on would be deflected through large angles. Thomson's and Rutherford's models are compared in Figure 2-4.

Bohr Sees the Light

Rutherford's Solar System Model did not last very long either because there was an *observation* that it could not explain: Light is radiated by atoms that have been excited by electrical discharges or that have received energy from other sources. You are undoubtedly familiar with such radiation—it is what is used to light neon signs, which are glass

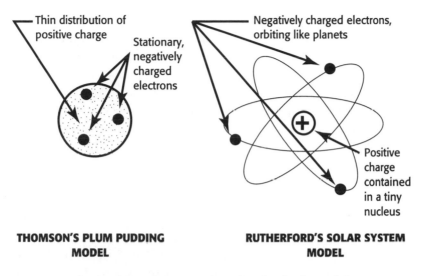

Thin distribution of positive charge

Stationary, negatively charged electrons

Negatively charged electrons, orbiting like planets

Positive charge contained in a tiny nucleus

THOMSON'S PLUM PUDDING MODEL

RUTHERFORD'S SOLAR SYSTEM MODEL

FIGURE 2-4. Comparison of Thomson's and Rutherford's Models

tubes filled with neon gas. When the electricity is turned on, the neon atoms are energized, returning some of this energy in the form of distinctly colored light.

The Solar System Model had no mechanism to account for such light, so a modification of this hypothesis had to be

made. In 1913, Niels Bohr, one of Rutherford's students, formulated a hypothesis that could account for the radiation of light. Bohr believed that electrons in atoms are restricted to certain circular orbits about the nucleus (only certain orbits are "allowed"). Each allowed orbit corresponds to an energy level for the electron. For hydrogen, the simplest atom, consisting of a nucleus and a single electron, Bohr's *hypothesis* was: The electron has a number of allowed orbits and allowed energy levels. When the atom receives energy from an outside source, like an electric current, it can accept only exactly the right amount of energy to send the electron from an allowed orbit of lower energy to an allowed orbit of higher energy. The electron lingers temporarily in this higher energy state, then jumps downward in energy, and eventually returns to the lowest energy level. The energy lost by the electron as it jumps down is given off as light, with the color of the light depending on the energy gap jumped by the electron.

Thus, the electron in a hydrogen atom behaves as if it is subject to the constraints experienced when being transported by an elevator. When you enter at the ground floor and punch a button, the elevator shoots up to the floor whose number you pushed. It then goes back down, stopping at other floors if other buttons are pushed, *but not between floors.* Eventually it returns to the lowest level. Rutherford's and Bohr's models are shown in Figure 2-5.

This hypothesis, with its restriction that only certain orbits and energy levels are allowed, might sound a bit strange. Bohr himself said: "We are all agreed the theory is crazy. The question that divides us is whether it is crazy enough to have a chance of being right." But right it seemed, for the hydrogen atom at least. The mathematical parts of this hypothesis allowed *predictions* to be made about the colors of light that would be expected to be given off when the electrons in hydrogen atoms lost energy jumping from each higher energy level to each lower energy level. When the *experiments* were carried out, the expected colors were seen. Thus, Bohr's hypothesis worked just fine

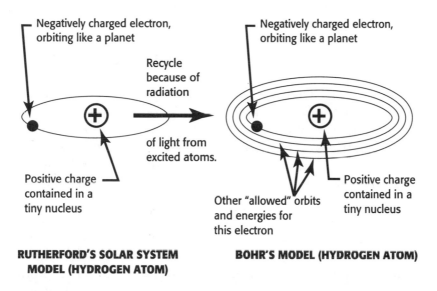

FIGURE 2-5. Rutherford's and Bohr's Models of the Hydrogen Atom

for the hydrogen atom. But what about all the other kinds of atoms?

Quantum Mechanics Dims the Light

Attempts were made to extend Bohr's *hypothesis* to atoms other than hydrogen. *Predictions* were made about the colors of light expected, and the corresponding *experiments* were carried out. Alas, the predicted colors were *not* found!

Once again the *recycling* of a scientific hypothesis was necessary. Bohr's hypothesis was eventually replaced by a much more complicated hypothesis that was developed over several decades by a number of physicists. It is referred to as the *Quantum Mechanical Model of the Atom*. *Quantum* refers to the smallest allowed increment of energy gained or lost at the atomic level by an electron. Quantum mechanics describes mathematically the properties of the electron when considered to behave as a wave or undulation, rather than as a particle.

The quantum mechanical hypothesis removes the specific orbits of the Bohr hypothesis, replacing them with a far more complicated mathematical structure that involves probabilities rather than specific locations of the electrons. The Quantum Mechanical Model says that the atom consists of a central nucleus containing protons (positive particles first observed in 1919) and neutrons (neutral particles discovered in 1932) together with electrons existing somewhere outside the nucleus and having definite allowed energies but no definite allowed orbits around the nucleus.

The absence of definite orbits means that it is not possible to determine both the position and velocity of the electron. Electrons can only be depicted as regions within which they have a high probability of being found. To help visualize "a region within which something has a high probability of being found," consider the barking, rain-predicting puppy, Domino, attached by a long rope to a stake in the middle of the lawn. Because he gets anxious when tied up, he's constantly on the move. To locate him, you need a way to observe him. This could be accomplished by using a camera to take snapshots from a vantage point above the lawn. Suppose further that, instead of being given individual photographic negatives, you were given the negatives piled on top of one another. If you were unable to separate the negatives, you could still look through the full stack to see a blend of Domino's locations. The longer he was in a certain location, the more intense his overall image would be at that location and the higher the probability of his being located in that region.

Heisenberg's Uncertainty

The removal of known, specific orbits for the electrons has been interpreted as meaning that there are limits to what can be observed, limits that are not dependent on the method of observation but are inherent in the nature of the matter itself. This notion was developed in 1927 by the Ger-

man physicist Werner Heisenberg. Heisenberg's uncertainty principle states that there are limits to the accuracy with which some properties of any particle can be known. There is no way of devising a method for pinpointing the exact position of the electrons in atoms without sacrificing some precision about how fast they are moving.

Although the random, unknowable feature of this theory might be philosophically difficult, scientists seem to be stuck with it until its predictions fail to be supported by experimental evidence. The test of the quantum mechanical model is "Does it work?" It does: Colors of light predicted by the Quantum Mechanical Model are actually seen in *experiments*. Bohr's model and the Quantum Mechanical Model are shown in Figure 2-6.

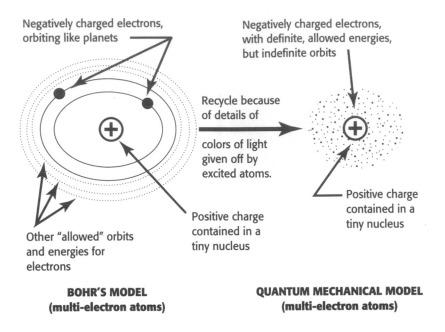

FIGURE 2-6. Bohr's and Quantum Mechanical Models of the Atom

Hark, Hark, a Quark!

Beginning in the 1930s, quantum mechanical atomic models became more complicated as additional subatomic particles were discovered. Soon dozens of presumably "elementary" particles were discovered, with every particle having an antiparticle.

In the 1960s, physicists theorized that many of these particles were composed of even tinier "seeds or prime units" called *quarks*. In the late 1960s, this theory was confirmed in an experiment similar to Rutherford's alpha-particle-scattering experiment. Just as Rutherford was not "looking for" the nucleus, Professors Kendall, Friedman, and Taylor were not "looking for" quarks. They shot electrons at protons in hydrogen atoms. Believing that the electric charge was distributed smoothly inside the proton, they predicted that the electrons would be scattered "softly" off the target protons, like a bullet passing through bread. The results of the experiment were a total surprise, for it was found that the electrons frequently scattered at wide angles, as shown in Figure 2-7. It was as though the electrons were encountering three small but very hard pieces. These pieces were eventually identified as quarks (two "up" quarks and one "down" quark).

Soon, four other types of quark had been proposed. According to the most recent model of the atom, the "standard model," there are twelve fundamental particles of matter: the six types of quark and six particles called *leptons,* a category including the electron.

The picture of the atom has changed considerably from that proposed by Democritus. There is, of course, no assurance that quarks and leptons are not made of yet smaller particles. The succession of models is shown in Figure 2-8.

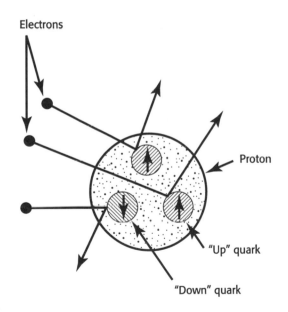

Electrons

Proton

"Up" quark

"Down" quark

Electrons deflect off the quarks.

FIGURE 2-7. Collisions with Quarks

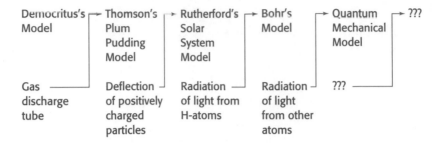

FIGURE 2-8. Evolution of Atom Models

Antiauthoritarianism

This exploration of atoms began with a competition between the authority of Aristotle and the authority of Democritus. In the modern scientific method, authority rests not in people, but in interpretation of experimental evidence. Although it is true that scientists might seem like authorities because they happen to know a lot about some particular phenomenon and that most people will leave it to others trained in the discipline of science to perform ex-

periments, hypotheses must be capable of being tested by anyone who is suitably trained.

Perhaps the essence of the method of science is that people do not have to take a scientist's word for his or her scientific statement. It is a reasoning process, and not a person, that is the final authority.

Idea Folders

5 Electromagnetic Radiation and Its Interaction with Matter

6 Wave Model versus Particle Model of Light

7 An Enlarged Atom: Flies Buzzing around Billiard Balls

8 Schrödinger's Cat: A Thought Experiment

9 Heisenberg's Uncertainty Principle

10 Matter versus Antimatter

11 Scanning Tunneling Microscopy: "Seeing" Atoms

12 The Four Basic Forces in Nature

13 Electricity and Magnetism: Siamese Twins

14 Newton's Laws of Motion and Gravitation

15 Einstein's Theories of Special and General Relativity

CHAPTER THREE

Big Idea #2

Chemistry's Periodic Law: Sorting the Elements

The true worth of a researcher lies in
pursuing what he did not seek in his
experiment as well as what he sought.

Claude Bernard

The earth, the seas, the breeze, the sun, the stars, and
everything else that you survey and can touch or be
touched by is matter. Matter can be as hard as steel, as
yielding as a pool of water, or as formless as the invisible
oxygen in the air. But whatever its form, whether solid or
liquid or gas, all matter is made of the same basic entities:
atoms. You have seen that within these atoms there is a
kind of order, with the nucleus containing uncharged neutrons and positively charged protons and with negatively
charged electrons dwelling in a hierarchy of energy levels
somewhere outside the nucleus.

Probing the Elements

Both physics and chemistry attempt to analyze atoms. Chemistry, however, deals not only with the structure of atoms, but also with the properties of those atoms—whether and how they combine with other atoms. Chemists deal with groups of atoms that they can sense (touch, smell, probe, manipulate). Groups of the same kind of atoms are called *elements*. Chemists have done all kinds of things to discover the properties of these elements—how they behave under various conditions. They have heated them, cooled them, mixed them, squeezed them, and they have observed. And the elements have reacted accordingly. Elements just do what comes naturally under particular circumstances. It is after observing how these elements behave that chemists formulate hypotheses about their nature.

Chemists' way of coming to understand the nature of elements is similar to the way you come to understand the nature of a new acquaintance: You observe how that individual behaves under a variety of conditions (stressful, tiring, joyful, and so on) and formulate a hypothesis about the possible nature of that person (wise, compassionate, unstable, secure, and so on). Your hypothesis is put to the test every time your expectations or predictions are matched with the person's behavior.

Universal Elements

Observation of different kinds of elements has been going on for a long time, but the modern understanding of elements—simple things from which complex structures are built—was long in coming. The ancient Greeks imagined that all things could be constructed from a single universal element: Thales (about 625–547 B.C.) thought that that element was water. Anaximenes (about 550 B.C.) thought it was air. Heraclitus (about 540–480 B.C.) thought it was fire, constantly changing form. Empedocles (about 490–430 B.C.) combined these hypotheses and added one more element to the list; according to him, earth, water, air, and fire could be combined to produce any substance. He explained the properties of wood, for example, as being solid like earth, producing fire, and giving off a vapor like air upon burning, with some of that vapor condensing to form drops of water. Aristotle (384–322 B.C.) added a fifth element, "aether," which comprised all of the universe outside of the Earth.

All this while, as was seen earlier, the Greeks had been reasoning without much experimentation. Centuries later, the Egyptians, who were a practical people, performed experiments that helped provide insight into the nature of matter. They heated rocks with charcoal to get metals, made glass from sand, and made bricks from clay. It is possible that the word *chemistry* is derived from "Chem," the Egyptians' name for their land. The word *chemia* came to be used to refer to treating metals to change their nature.

In the second century B.C., Bolos of Mendes, an Egyptian, tried to combine the practical knowledge of the Egyptians with the Greeks' hypothesis about universal elements. He had *observed* that it was possible to combine substances (e.g., copper and zinc) to produce a new substance that looked like gold. (That substance was brass, an alloy, or mixture, of metals.) Reasoning from the Greeks' *hypothesis,* which stated that any substance is simply a combination of the universal elements, he *predicted* that gold, that most highly prized metal, could be produced if the appropriate universal elements were mixed in the right proportions.

Alchemy: Big Failure/Bigger Success

In the centuries that followed Bolos of Mendes's efforts, alchemists, the medieval forerunners of chemists, formulated recipes for gold and conducted the corresponding *experiments.* Much to their disappointment, Bolos's prediction was never borne out. *Transmutation,* which is the conversion of one element to another, was never achieved by mixing substances with each other. (It *has* been accomplished by altering the nuclei of atoms, as you will soon see.) All this

"FRANKLY, I'D BE SATISFIED NOW IF I COULD EVEN TURN GOLD INTO LEAD."

cookery was not, however, a complete failure. These experiments contributed to the advance of science by helping develop new scientific techniques and new materials. The alchemists' results served later as observations leading to more valid hypotheses.

The Elements' Atomic Masses

While nineteenth-century physicists were probing the inner workings of the atom, chemists were busy cataloging the behavior of as many different kinds of elements as they could get their hands on. By about 1869, approximately sixty elements were known. Studies had been made of their physical properties, such as boiling point, melting point, density, and so on, as well as their chemical properties (how they react with other elements). Chemists had observed that some of the elements reacted quite readily, whereas others were sluggish and still others did not seem to get involved at all—just like people! Furthermore, certain patterns were becoming apparent. There were groups of elements that exhibited similar chemical properties; for example, elements in a given group would all react with one particular element to produce the same kind of compound.

Nineteenth-century chemists had determined the atomic mass of each element—a physical property that is a measure of the mass of an atom of one element compared to the mass of an atom of another element. The lowest atomic mass, about 1, belonged to the element hydrogen (H). (Chemists abbreviate the names of the elements with one or two letters.) Next, according to the observations of that day, came the following elements, given with their approximate atomic masses:

lithium (Li), 7
beryllium (Be), 9
boron (B), 11
carbon (C), 12
nitrogen (N), 14
oxygen (O), 16
fluorine (F), 19
sodium (Na), 23
magnesium (Mg), 24

aluminum (Al), 27
silicon (Si), 28
phosphorus (P), 31
sulfur (S), 32
chlorine (Cl), 35
potassium (K), 39
calcium (Ca), 40
titanium (Ti), 48

And so on.

Repeat Performances

Prior to 1869, chemists had sought relationships between atomic masses and chemical properties but had met with only limited success. In 1817 and 1829, Johann Dobereiner published articles in which he examined the properties of sets of elements that he called *triads* (for example, lithium, sodium, and potassium). The elements of each triad have similar chemical properties, and the atomic mass of the second element of the triad is approximately equal to the average of the atomic masses of the other two elements. This attempt failed to provide a comprehensive framework. In the years 1863 to 1866, John Newlands proposed his law of octaves. Newlands stated that when the elements are listed in increasing atomic mass, the eighth element is similar in chemical properties to the first, the ninth to the second, and so on, just like notes in musical octaves. Newlands carried the idea of the metaphor too far; the actual relationship is not so simple. His work was not taken seriously by other chemists.

In 1869, a Russian chemist, Dimitri Mendeleev, decided to arrange the elements in horizontal rows of increasing atomic masses (see Figure 3-1). The lightest element, hydrogen, was the sole member of the first row. The second row began with lithium and continued until fluorine. When he reached the next element, sodium, an element whose properties were quite similar to those of lithium (e.g., reacting violently with water), he started a new row, placing

H 1 Hydrogen						
Li 7 Lithium	Be 9 Beryllium	B 11 Boron	C 12 Carbon	N 14 Nitrogen	O 16 Oxygen	F 19 Fluorine
Na 23 Sodium	Mg 24 Magnesium	Al 27 Aluminum	Si 28 Silicon	P 31 Phosphorus	S 32 Sulfur	Cl 35 Chlorine
K 39 Potassium	Ca 40 Calcium					

FIGURE 3-1. Mendeleev's Periodic Table: Elements and Their Atomic Masses (rounded off to the nearest whole number)

sodium below lithium. He continued along this row until the pattern repeated, with potassium (which also reacted violently with water) being placed below sodium. Next, he placed calcium below magnesium and beryllium.

The table that was produced showed elements in horizontal rows, or periods, of increasing atomic mass. The elements in the same vertical column were members of groups with similar chemical properties. When arranged in this fashion, a pattern emerged: The chemical properties of the elements were recurring in a periodic fashion. After the period begun by lithium and terminated by fluorine, the chemical properties of lithium were encountered again in the next periods with the elements sodium and potassium; beryllium's chemical properties (e.g., reaction with oxygen to produce a white solid compound that reacts slowly with water) were encountered again with magnesium and calcium; and so on.

Filling the Gaps

After calcium, the next known element in order of atomic mass was titanium. If Mendeleev placed titanium immediately following calcium, it would occupy a place directly below aluminum. But he knew from his study of the chemical properties of boron and aluminum that titanium did not fit into that group: Boron and aluminum form compounds with oxygen in which the ratio of boron or aluminum atoms to oxygen atoms is two to three. Using subscripts to indicate the relative number of atoms, these compounds can be represented by the formula E_2O_3, where "E" represents an element in the boron-aluminum group. Titanium forms a compound with oxygen whose general formula corresponds to that of the carbon-silicon group, namely, EO_2. Because titanium's chemical properties more closely matched those of the elements in the carbon-silicon group than those in the boron-aluminum group, Mendeleev boldly skipped one space, placing titanium below silicon, as shown in Figure 3-2.

H 1 Hydrogen						
Li 7 Lithium	Be 9 Beryllium	B 11 Boron	C 12 Carbon	N 14 Nitrogen	O 16 Oxygen	F 19 Fluorine
Na 23 Sodium	Mg 24 Magnesium	Al 27 Aluminum	Si 28 Silicon	P 31 Phosphorus	S 32 Sulfur	Cl 35 Chlorine
K 39 Potassium	Ca 40 Calcium		Ti 48 Titanium			

FIGURE 3-2. Placement of Titanium in the Periodic Table

This space or gap was really a prediction. Mendeleev's hypothesis was that the chemical properties of the elements recur in a periodic fashion or, more specifically, that the chemical properties of the elements are periodic functions of their atomic masses. Based on this hypothesis, Mendeleev predicted that another element should exist that fits the blank space in the periodic array of elements. This element should have properties similar to boron and aluminum and should have an atomic mass between those of calcium (40) and titanium (48). His prediction was found to be correct when scandium (Sc), atomic mass 45, was discovered in 1879 (see Figure 3-3).

In time, many other gaps left by Mendeleev in his periodic table of elements were also filled. His predictions of the properties of these missing elements were so accurate that they provided further credibility for his hypothesis.

Mendeleev was not the first to recognize that, when the elements are listed in order of increasing atomic mass, elements with similar chemical properties appear at fairly regular intervals. He was, however, the first to break from *rigid adherence* to the hypothesis that the chemical properties of the elements are periodic functions of their atomic masses.

H 1 Hydrogen						
Li 7 Lithium	Be 9 Beryllium	B 11 Boron	C 12 Carbon	N 14 Nitrogen	O 16 Oxygen	F 19 Fluorine
Na 23 Sodium	Mg 24 Magnesium	Al 27 Aluminum	Si 28 Silicon	P 31 Phosphorus	S 32 Sulfur	Cl 35 Chlorine
K 39 Potassium	Ca 40 Calcium	Sc 45 Scandium	Ti 48 Titanium			

Figure 3-3. Placement of Scandium in the Periodic Table

That rigid adherence caused several difficulties. One problem was the placement of the elements iodine (I), atomic mass 127, and tellurium (Te), atomic mass 128. If placed in order of increasing atomic mass, iodine would fall into the group consisting of oxygen, sulfur, and selenium (Se), and tellurium would fall into the group consisting of fluorine, chlorine, and bromine (Br). That did not make sense in terms of the chemical properties of the two elements: Iodine's properties most closely resembled those of the fluorine-chlorine-bromine group, whereas tellurium's best fit the oxygen-sulfur-selenium group. Mendeleev chose to ignore the succession of atomic masses here and to place them according to similarities in chemical properties (see Figure 3-4).

Group properties can help explain many phenomena. Look at calcium (Ca) and strontium (Sr), for example. They are members of the same group and have similar properties. Fallout from atmospheric nuclear testing contains radioactive strontium. When ingested by humans, mainly in milk, strontium can take the place of calcium in bones and induce bone cancer and leukemia.

H 1 Hydrogen						
Li 7 Lithium	Be 9 Beryllium	B 11 Boron	C 12 Carbon	N 14 Nitrogen	O 16 Oxygen	F 19 Fluorine
Na 23 Sodium	Mg 24 Magnesium	Al 27 Aluminum	Si 28 Silicon	P 31 Phosphorus	S 32 Sulfur	Cl 35 Chlorine
K 39 Potassium	Ca 40 Calcium	Sc 45 Scandium	Ti 48 Titanium		Se 79 Selenium	Br 80 Bromine
					Te 128 Tellurium	I 127 Iodine

Figure 3-4. Placement of Tellurium and Iodine in the Periodic Table

Atomic Numbers to the Rescue

A measure unknown in Mendeleev's time is the *atomic number*—the number of protons in the nucleus of an atom. It is a more fundamental guide to correlating chemical properties than atomic mass is. In its modern form, the periodic law can be stated: The chemical properties of the elements are periodic functions of their atomic numbers. Tellurium, atomic number 52, thus precedes iodine, atomic number 53 (see Figure 3-5). In a sense, Mendeleev was lucky, for increasing atomic mass is almost always correlated with increasing atomic number.

Room to Grow

The number of known elements has increased greatly since the days of the ancient Greeks. There are now about 112 known elements, each of which is described quite well by

1							
H							
1							
Hydrogen							

3	4	5	6	7	8	9
Li	Be	B	C	N	O	F
7	9	11	12	14	16	19
Lithium	Beryllium	Boron	Carbon	Nitrogen	Oxygen	Fluorine

11	12	13	14	15	16	17
Na	Mg	Al	Si	P	S	Cl
23	24	27	28	31	32	35
Sodium	Magnesium	Aluminum	Silicon	Phosphorus	Sulfur	Chlorine

19	20	21	22		34	35
K	Ca	Sc	Ti		Se	Br
39	40	45	48		79	80
Potassium	Calcium	Scandium	Titanium		Selenium	Bromine

		52	53
Note: Atomic numbers are shown above element symbols; atomic masses below.		Te	I
		128	127
		Tellurium	Iodine

FIGURE 3-5. Amended Version of the Periodic Table, Including Atomic Numbers above Symbols

the periodic law. In order to accommodate all of these elements, the periodic table has been modified in form and expanded (see Figure 3-6). As a result, scandium is no longer placed under boron and aluminum, and titanium is no longer located under carbon and silicon.

"THE PERIODIC TABLE."

atomic number →
atomic mass →

1
H
1.0079

1	2	3	4	5	6	7	8	9	10	11	12	13	14	15	16	17	18
1 **H** 1.0079																	2 **He** 4.00260
3 **Li** 6.941	4 **Be** 9.01218											5 **B** 10.81	6 **C** 12.011	7 **N** 14.0067	8 **O** 15.9994	9 **F** 18.99840	10 **Ne** 20.179
11 **Na** 22.98977	12 **Mg** 24.305											13 **Al** 26.98154	14 **Si** 28.0855	15 **P** 30.97376	16 **S** 32.06	17 **Cl** 35.433	18 **Ar** 39.948
19 **K** 39.0983	20 **Ca** 40.08	21 **Sc** 44.9559	22 **Ti** 47.88	23 **V** 50.9415	24 **Cr** 51.996	25 **Mn** 54.9380	26 **Fe** 55.847	27 **Co** 58.9332	28 **Ni** 58.69	29 **Cu** 63.546	30 **Zn** 65.38	31 **Ga** 69.72	32 **Ge** 72.59	33 **As** 74.9216	34 **Se** 78.96	35 **Br** 79.904	36 **Kr** 83.80
37 **Rb** 85.4678	38 **Sr** 87.62	39 **Y** 88.9059	40 **Zr** 91.22	41 **Nb** 92.9064	42 **Mo** 95.94	43 **Tc** 98.9072	44 **Ru** 101.07	45 **Rh** 102.9055	46 **Pd** 106.42	47 **Ag** 107.868	48 **Cd** 112.41	49 **In** 114.82	50 **Sn** 118.69	51 **Sb** 121.75	52 **Te** 127.60	53 **I** 126.9045	54 **Xe** 131.29
55 **Cs** 132.9054	56 **Ba** 137.34	57* **La** 138.9055	72 **Hf** 178.49	73 **Ta** 180.9479	74 **W** 183.85	75 **Re** 186.207	76 **Os** 190.2	77 **Ir** 192.22	78 **Pt** 195.08	79 **Au** 196.9665	80 **Hg** 200.59	81 **Tl** 204.383	82 **Pb** 207.2	83 **Bi** 208.9804	84 **Po** (209)	85 **At** (210)	86 **Rn** (222)
87 **Fr** (223)	88 **Ra** 226.0254	89** **Ac** 227.0278	104 **Unq** 261.11	105 **Unp** 262.114	106 **Unh** 263.118	107 **Uns** 262.12	108 **Uno** (265)	109 **Une** (266)	110 **Uun**	111 **Uuu**	112 **Uub**						

*
58 **Ce** 140.12	59 **Pr** 140.9077	60 **Nd** 144.24	61 **Pm** (145)	62 **Sm** 150.36	63 **Eu** 151.96	64 **Gd** 157.25	65 **Tb** 158.9254	66 **Dy** 162.50	67 **Ho** 164.9304	68 **Er** 16726	69 **Tm** 168.9342	70 **Yb** 173.04	71 **Lu** 174.967

**
90 **Th** 232.0381	91 **Pa** 231.0359	92 **U** 238.029	93 **Np** 237.0482	94 **Pu** (244)	95 **Am** 243.0614	96 **Cm** (247)	97 **Bk** (247)	98 **Cf** (251)	99 **Es** 252.083	100 **Fm** 259.0951	101 **Md** (258)	102 **No** 259.1009	103 **Lr** 262.11

FIGURE 3-6. Modern Periodic Table.

The great explanatory and predictive power of the periodic law makes it a really big idea. It has been used not only to make predictions about the existence of elements to fill gaps within the periodic table, but also to make predictions about elements whose atomic numbers are beyond those presently known.

In a sense, there is a huge gap at the tail end of the periodic arrangement. Scientists all over the globe are competing with each other for the distinction of filling this gap. They test the periodic law each time they synthesize a new element and study the new element's properties in relation to its position in the table.

Element Recycling

To create new elements, new nuclei must be made. Alteration of the number of protons in the nucleus of an atom converts that atom into an atom of another element. To represent these processes in symbolic form, the atomic number (number of protons) is indicated at the lower left-hand corner of the symbol of the element, and the atomic mass (number of protons plus neutrons) at the upper left-hand corner. For example, a carbon atom, atomic number 6, that contains 6 neutrons is represented as $^{12}_{6}C$; and a proton (which is identical to a hydrogen nucleus containing no neutrons) is represented as $^{1}_{1}H$. If the carbon atom and the proton are combined, or fused together, the resulting nucleus contains a total of 7 protons and 6 neutrons. Because its atomic number is 7, it is the element nitrogen. Because it has 7 protons and 6 neutrons, its atomic mass is 13. The reaction between the carbon nucleus and the proton can be shown as:

$$^{12}_{6}C + ^{1}_{1}H \rightarrow ^{13}_{7}N$$

Note that the sum of the lower numbers on the left side of the arrow (6 and 1) is the same as the lower number on the right side of the arrow (7) and that the sum of the upper numbers on the left side of the arrow (12 and 1) is the same as the upper number on the right side of the arrow (13).

Atoms that have the same number of protons but differ from each other in the number of neutrons are called *isotopes*. Isotopes are like some identical twins—not *exactly* identical. All nitrogen atoms have 7 protons, but some have 6 neutrons, some have 7, and so on. The isotope of nitrogen produced by the fusion of $^{12}_{6}C$ and $^{1}_{1}H$ is called *nitrogen-13*.

Alteration of the number of neutrons (n) in the nucleus converts an atom of an element to an isotope of that element. In the following example, uranium-239, an isotope of uranium (U), is produced:

$$^{238}_{92}U + ^{1}_{0}n \rightarrow ^{239}_{92}U$$

Isotopes produced by this technique are often radioactive and decay to form new elements—uranium-239 decays to produce an isotope of neptunium (Np), neptunium-239, and an electron (e):

$$^{239}_{92}U \rightarrow ^{239}_{93}Np + ^{0}_{-1}e$$

Nuclear transformation has enabled modern chemists to realize Bolos of Mendes's dream of the transmutation of elements—even gold (Au) can be produced by this new alchemy, as when certain platinum (Pt) isotopes decay:

$$^{197}_{78}Pt \rightarrow ^{197}_{79}Au + ^{0}_{-1}e$$

Such gold will not flood the market, however, because of the expense involved in its production and because platinum has a higher market value!

The Name Game

Until recently, the group that first synthesized an element got the privilege of naming it.

In 1979, a new naming policy was adopted because of a conflict involved in deciding who first synthesized element

104. American scientists and Russian scientists both laid claim to this honor. The Americans chose to call the new element rutherfordium (Rf) after Ernest Rutherford, whereas the Russians chose to call it kurchatovium (Ku) after the Russian physicist Igor Kurchatov. These claims for the discovery and naming of element 104 were studied by the International Union of Pure and Applied Chemistry (IUPAC), the arbitrator in such matters. Instead of deciding in favor of either nation, the IUPAC decreed that the new element be named unnilquadium (un = 1, nil = 0, quad = 4). Thus, element 105 would be unnilquintium, element 106 unnilhexium, and so on. How dullium!

In 1994, the IUPAC relented. It recommended naming element 104 and other unnamed elements after deceased scientists or locations where new elements have been synthesized. As a kind of compromise, element 104 was dubbed neither rutherfordium nor kurchatovium, but dubnium (Db), after Dubna where the Russians made that element. Rutherford will be honored by the naming of element 106 rutherfordium.

Conflicts about a weapons race are being replaced by conflicts about an elements race. Now *that's* progress!

Idea Folders

 Radioisotopes as Tracers

17 Organic versus Inorganic Chemistry

CHAPTER FOUR

Big Idea #3

Astronomy's Big Bang Theory: Tracing the Elements' Roots

I don't pretend to understand the universe,
it is a great deal bigger than I am.

Thomas Carlyle

Now to proceed all the way from the world of the very small to the unimaginably large world of the universe itself. Measured against the vastness of the universe, human beings may seem puny. Awe is appropriate, but do not feel overawed. Although the universe contains huge masses and large spaces, the very fact that you can discuss and understand any of it suggests that you have some remarkable talents.

What's Going on Out There, And How Long Has It Been Going On?

Observations of the celestial bodies that make up the universe have been plentiful. People can readily see the sun and other stars and even some planets. Scientists have observed planet Earth, and through telescope and space probes, other planets in the solar system. They have charted galaxies (collections of stars) and even clusters of galaxies. Based on these observations, astronomers attempt to describe the universe and to figure out how long it took to reach its present state.

The current estimate for the age of the universe is between 10 and 20 billion years. Because people have been making and recording careful, systematic, quantitative observations of the universe for about only a thousand years, the time spent in observation is an extremely small fraction of the total time involved. In spite of this limitation, astronomers have been able to formulate highly detailed hypotheses about the universe.

How to Shift the Center of the Universe

The earliest hypotheses depicted all the items in the universe in terms of their relationship to the Earth. These geocentric (*geo* = Earth) models of the universe placed the Earth at the center of the universe. This corresponded nicely with religious beliefs and was taught and generally believed until the 1500s. According to this theory, the universe is homocentric: Humankind is at its center.

A major geocentric hypothesis was called the Ptolemaic theory (after Claudius Ptolemeus, who perfected it in A.D. 140). According to this theory, the moon, sun, planets, and stars revolve in circular orbits about the Earth, which is stationary and located in the center of the universe. This hypothesis accounted for all the then-known facts about the solar system. Moreover, it could be used to make fairly accurate predictions of planetary positions.

Many centuries later, in 1543, Copernicus's study of the Earth, moon, sun, planets, and stars led him to a radically different model of the universe. According to the Copernican theory of the universe, the stars were fixed, and the Earth and other planets orbited the sun. Because of the

"HE HAS A PRE-COPERNICAN ATTITUDE ABOUT HIMSELF — BELIEVES HE'S THE CENTER OF THE UNIVERSE."

fixed position of the sun, this is referred to as a *heliocentric model* of the universe (*helio* = sun). Many people rejected the heliocentric model because it was *nonhomocentric*—humankind was no longer the focal point of the universe.

Later, Galileo was able to obtain telescopic evidence that helped decide between the two theories. In the Copernican view, Venus should go through all phases, just like the Earth's moon. In the Ptolemaic view, it should not. When Galileo, using one of the first astronomical telescopes, observed that Venus did go through all phases he knew that the Ptolemaic hypothesis had to be incorrect. Earth-centered chauvinism eventually gave way to a nonhomocentric perspective.

A Really Big Bang

The Copernican theory focused on a relatively small portion of the universe. It is now known that myriad celestial bodies populate its vast reaches. Modern hypotheses about the universe are more comprehensive and dynamic in nature. They cover a wider range and describe constant change. They seek to describe the past, present, and future of the universe.

The modern view of the universe was formulated after the American astronomer Edwin Hubble made a landmark observation in 1929. Hubble observed in the light from other galaxies that the distinctive colors emitted by the various elements they contained were different from those emitted by those same elements on Earth. These neon-signs-in-the-sky had colors that had been *redshifted*—moved toward the red end of the violet-indigo-blue-green-yellow-orange-red spectrum; a violet color emitted by an atom on Earth might appear as indigo when emitted in a distant galaxy and then seen on Earth.

You might have observed a similar effect in the changing pitch of a horn or whistle on a moving car or train: The pitch of the sound gets higher when the vehicle approaches you and gets lower as it passes you. Just as a drop in pitch indicates a receding sound source, a redshift indicates a receding light source. Hubble concluded that virtually all galaxies seem to be moving away from Earth. In other words, the universe is expanding.

This dynamic situation can be envisioned by imagining a slightly inflated balloon covered with dots. Each dot represents a galaxy. If you place yourself on a single dot on the surface of this balloon and then further inflate the balloon, all the other dots appear to be moving away from your position and from all other dots. (In this analogy, in addition to the overall expansion, each dot on the balloon is itself expanding. This is not true in the universe—galaxies are not generally expanding internally.)

If every galaxy—or, more accurately, every cluster of galaxies—is moving away from every other one now, it would seem reasonable to hypothesize that, at an earlier time, galaxies must have been closer together. In fact, carried to its extreme, it can be hypothesized that, at one time, all the matter of the universe was together. Because it is now known how far apart the galaxies are and approximately how fast they are moving, it has been possible to estimate that this single unit existed about 15 billion years ago.

"THE ONLY PART OF THE UNIVERSE WHICH ISN'T EXPANDING IS THE BUDGET FOR THIS PLACE."

If there was once a single unit containing all the matter of the universe and if that unit began expanding, it is possible to imagine some kind of explosion taking place. This is the starting point of the most widely accepted theory about the origin of the universe: the Big Bang theory. (Who says theories have to have fancy names!) The original unit, called the *primeval fireball,* must have been unimaginably hot and extremely tightly packed. Things were so hot in the primeval fireball that neither atoms nor even protons, neutrons, or electrons could exist.

For reasons that are not at all clear, the primeval fireball blew up—BANG!—scattering its material in all directions. The temperature decrease that resulted from the expansion permitted the "freezing" of quarks into protons and

neutrons, much as water freezes into ice when the temperature drops to 0°C. Subsequent temperature decreases permitted the freezing of nuclei and then atoms.

This expansion has some unique and mind-boggling characteristics: Ordinary expansions occur *in* space—they fill more space. By contrast, the Big Bang was an explosion *of* space, not *in* space. Space itself *was created* in the Big Bang.

Another fascinating aspect of a universe created by a Big Bang is that it has no center and no edge. To help with this thought, consider the surface of the expanding balloon mentioned earlier. Where is the center of the surface of that balloon? There *is* no center—every point on the surface is at the *same* vantage point relative to the overall surface.

Was There Really a Big Bang?

To decide whether there was a Big Bang, consider a few predictions made on the basis of this theory. One prediction is based on the notion that during the first few minutes of the expansion, conditions were suitable for fusion reactions involving protons (hydrogen nuclei) and neutrons. The major end products of these reactions were helium nuclei (which contain two protons). The overall composition of the expanding fireball—of the universe—was determined during those first few minutes.

PREDICTION 1 Calculations based on these reactions indicate that the universe should be about 25 percent helium.

EXPERIMENT 1 Most large astronomical objects whose chemical composition is known are between 23 and 27 percent helium.

A second prediction is based on the fact that energy accompanies explosions. The Big Bang, therefore, should have flooded the entire universe with very intense radiation energy. With the expansion of the universe, the intensity of this radiation must have decreased, but traces of such background radiation or "echo" of the Big Bang should be detectable.

PREDICTION 2 Cosmic background radiation, a kind of fossil remnant of the Big Bang, should be found throughout the universe.

EXPERIMENT 2 Background radiation in the form of microwaves (originally thought to be excess static in a 1965 experiment conducted at Bell Telephone Laboratories) was shown to correspond to that predicted by the Big Bang theory. These radio waves come from *all* directions in the sky. This is to be expected because, as was stated, the Big Bang happened *everywhere,* creating and filling the whole universe.

Element Factories

So, the Big Bang theory can explain how the universe as a whole might have developed and how a small variety of nuclei might have been produced. How then did the wide variety of elements within this universe develop? The answer lies in the stars.

After the primeval fireball exploded, it did not evolve in a completely uniform fashion. Rather, there were localized concentrations of protons, neutrons, electrons, and small nuclei such as helium that blew out in various directions. These lumps or gas clouds are quite typical of explosions. If you have ever dropped a glass of milk or a jar of sour cream, you know that globs of various size and shape are produced in the expansion.

Within gas clouds, protons, neutrons, and helium and other nuclei can attract each other gravitationally, just as Earth gravitationally attracts the items on it. As a result, the gas clouds can contract as the particles move closer together (see Figure 4-1).

If the gas cloud contains a sufficiently large number of particles, the material can become highly compressed. Eventually the protons, neutrons, and helium nuclei get close enough to undergo a process called *nuclear fusion*—smaller nuclei coalesce to form larger nuclei, giving off energy in the process. For example, two hydrogen-1 nuclei (protons), $_1^1H$, can fuse together to form a new isotope, hydrogen-2, $_1^2H$. In

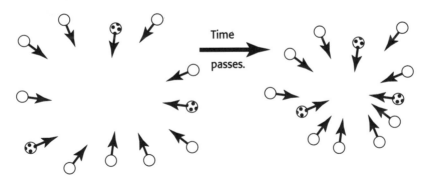

Cloud of hydrogen and helium is blown out of the primeval fireball.

Cloud condenses because of gravitational attraction.

Figure 4-1. Contraction of a Gas Cloud of Matter from the Primeval Fireball.

the process, a positron (positive electron), $_1^0e$, and energy are also produced:

$$_1^1H + _1^1H \rightarrow _1^2H + _1^0e + energy$$

These two isotopes of hydrogen can then fuse together to form a new element, helium-3, $_2^3He$.

$$_1^1H + _1^2H \rightarrow _2^3He + energy$$

Two atoms of the helium-3 produced can fuse together to form helium-4, $_2^4He$, plus two protons:

$$_2^3He + _2^3He \rightarrow _2^4He + 2_1^1H + energy$$

The helium-4 thus produced can fuse with helium-3 to produce another new element, beryllium-7, $_4^7Be$:

$$_2^3He + _2^4He \rightarrow _4^7Be + energy$$

The fusion process can continue, ultimately producing many of the elements in the periodic table. These large gas clouds that support nuclear fusion are called *stars* and are shown in Figure 4-2.

Thus, a star is an element factory in which energy is produced as more massive nuclei are synthesized. Galaxies are collections of stars held together by the forces of mutual gravitational attraction. The first galaxy is thought to have formed about 2 billion years after the Big Bang.

Superstars

Eventually, the process of nuclear fusion uses up much of the star's fuel—the smaller nuclei from which larger nuclei are manufactured—and the star's life nears its end. Without enough nuclear fuel to keep the star's temperature and internal pressure sufficiently high, the star begins to contract.

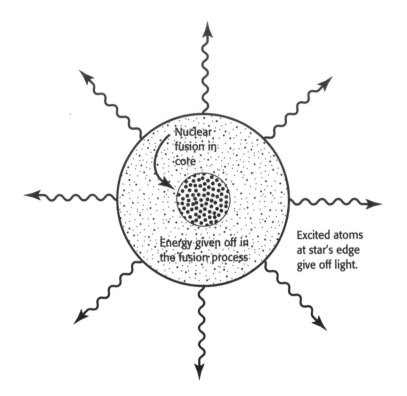

FIGURE 4-2. Star Dynamics

This gravitational collapse results in rapid heating as the particles crash into each other with great force and create even larger nuclei. For stars of ordinary mass, the result can be the formation of an expanded star called a *red giant*. In the case of a supermassive star, there is a catastrophic explosion that astronomers call a *supernova*, as shown in Figure 4-3.

A recent supernova observation was made in 1987. The star went out with a bang, ejecting its outer layers into space. These layers contain larger nuclei that the star created in its death. This enriched material can be incorporated into new generations of stars. The sun contains many of the nuclei in the periodic table, so the sun is at least a second-generation star, formed perhaps 4 to 5 billion years ago.

"IT'S SOMEWHERE BETWEEN A NOVA AND A SUPERNOVA...PROBABLY A PRETTY GOOD NOVA."

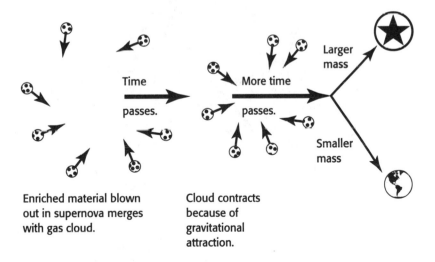

Time passes.

More time passes.

Larger mass

Smaller mass

Enriched material blown out in supernova merges with gas cloud.

Cloud contracts because of gravitational attraction.

FIGURE 4-3. Possibilities of What Might Happen to Enriched Material Blown Out in a Supernova

Hypotheses within Hypotheses

Included within the Big Bang hypothesis is the idea that the sun, Earth, and other planets in the solar system were formed from a relatively small enriched gas cloud called a *nebula*. According to this *nebular hypothesis,* the sun and planets of the solar system began as a large, diffuse, slowly rotating cloud of gas that gradually contracted under the influence of its own gravitational field. As it began to spin faster (like a spinning ice skater who draws her arms in closer to her sides), a series of rings formed around the equator of the shrinking cloud of gas. The central mass, heated by gravitational contraction that set off nuclear fusion, became the sun. Rings of material left behind by the shrinking sun-to-be coalesced to form planets.

"WE'VE DISCOVERED A MASSIVE DUST AND GAS CLOUD WHICH IS EITHER THE BEGINNING OF A NEW STAR OR JUST A HELL OF A LOT OF DUST AND GAS."

Cosmic Linkages

The primeval fireball was too hot for the more massive nuclei to form. Gas clouds blown from the Big Bang contracted because of gravitational attraction, forming stars, which built the nuclei of new elements by nuclear fusion. Supernovae resulting from explosions of some of these stars produced stars containing collections of these new elements. Planets might have formed from contracting enriched gas clouds blown out of a large star containing a large variety of elements.

This is quite a cosmic linkage. The whole Earth, including its human residents, consists of atoms whose nuclei were formed in the searing hot core of a gigantic star that exploded billions of years ago. We are truly children of the stars!

Big Chill or Big Crunch?

The Big Bang theory is based on beliefs about the universe's past development. But what of the future? Where does it go from here? This is the biggest question in astronomy today, and the answer is not clear.

Two competing theories are illustrated in Figure 4-4: (1) In the continued expansion theory, the universe will keep on moving outward without reaching any limit (a Big Chill). (2) In the oscillating universe theory, the expansion will reach a limit (a maximum volume) and then will reverse the process by undergoing billions of years of contraction (a Big Crunch) until, finally, the primeval fireball might be reformed—and explode again!

There is a prediction/experiment sequence that could decide between these two theories: Not all rocket ships are successful in escaping the Earth's gravitational field. If a rocket ship departs from the Earth's surface, whether it continues "expanding" from the Earth or ceases its upward motion, reverses direction, and comes back will depend on

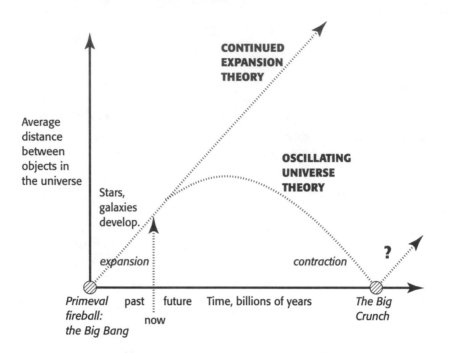

FIGURE 4-4. The Universe—Past, Present, and Future

how fast the rocket is moving and how large is the gravitational force pulling it back to Earth. A gravitational force that is more powerful than the force generated by the rocket's engines will make the rocket eventually return to Earth.

The gravitational force between objects depends upon the masses of those objects—the greater the masses, the greater the force of attraction. If the gravitational force among all the matter in the universe is great enough (if the mass of the universe is great enough), the force will eventually be able to pull all the universe matter back together again. If the gravitational force is not great enough (if the mass is not great enough), the universe will continue expanding. Thus, the fate of the universe is determined by its mass.

"THAT WRAPS IT UP—THE MASS OF THE UNIVERSE."

PREDICTION According to the oscillating universe theory, the mass of the universe is greater than *a critical amount calculated by astronomers*, the amount needed for gravity to pull all the matter of the universe back together.

EXPERIMENT The sum of all the masses actually observed by astronomers is only about 1 percent of the critical mass that they have calculated. By adding the masses of additional matter inferred from the motion of galaxies, this figure increases to 10 to 30 percent of the critical mass—still well below that required for eventual contraction.

Seeing in the Dark

The question of the universe's future is not settled just from observed matter. Could the universe contain matter not yet detected by astronomers? A very good case can be made for the existence of other objects, for example, *black holes*—massive bodies that are thought to be remnants of burned-out large stars. While substantial material is blown out in the supernova explosion that ends a large star's life, even more material implodes, possibly crushing itself either into a very dense *neutron star* (in which matter is so compressed that protons and electrons are absent) or into a black hole.

Black holes contain enormously large quantities of matter, densely packed into an extremely small space. As a result, a black hole's gravitational attraction is so strong that even light cannot escape! This makes the black hole invisible.

To understand why light cannot escape from black holes, think about a space vehicle blasting off from the moon. To leave the moon's surface, astronauts only needed to use a relatively small rocket, which gave them sufficient speed to escape the moon's gravity. To escape the more massive Earth's gravity, a more powerful rocket was required for greater speed. A black hole is so massive that even light, which travels at the fastest known speed, does not travel fast enough to escape.

Astronomers already have evidence for the possible existence of several black holes, one of which may be at the center of the Milky Way galaxy. The total mass of the universe, then, cannot be estimated accurately without knowing how many black holes exist, how much matter is contained in these black holes, and also how much matter might exist in so-called "dark matter," material that cannot be observed by telescopes.

But Where Did It All Come From?

Note that both the Big Bang and the oscillating universe theories are silent about where the primeval fireball came

"THE LAST I HEARD, MEDWICK WAS WORKING ON A MODEL 'BLACK HOLE' IN HIS LABORATORY."

from—and, for that matter, why it blew up. The method of science is a handy tool, but it only goes so far. In the beginning, did there suddenly come into existence a primeval

COSMOLOGY MARCHES ON

fireball, or has it been around in some form for all eternity? Did it come out of nowhere, or was it always there? It reminds one of that ancient query: Has God always existed or did God somehow come into being? Who made God?

St. Augustine's answer to the question "What was God doing before He created Heaven and Earth?" was, "He was preparing a Hell for those who inquire into such matters!"

Idea Folders

18 A Relatively Short Observation Time

19 Visible versus Nonvisible Astronomies

20 Estimating the Age of the Universe

21 The Missing Mass Problem

22 Black Holes, White Holes, Worm Holes

CHAPTER FIVE

Big Idea #4

Geology's Plate Tectonics Model: Down to Earth

The longer the island of knowledge, the
longer the shoreline of wonder.

Ralph W. Sockman

So far, you have gone from models of atoms all the way to theories about the genesis of the entire universe. Now, plant your feet firmly on Earth and see how another of the branches of science—geology—has applied the method of science to some aspects of your home planet.

Geologists have had much direct experience with the Earth's surface, but there are still a few portions of the land surface and major portions of the undersea area that remain unexplored. Their experience with Earth's interior is considerably less extensive. Drillers have only penetrated about 12 kilometers of the Earth's 6,000-plus-kilometer radius. Nevertheless, although they have barely scratched the surface, geologists have a pretty good idea of what is inside. This giant black box called Earth has been penetrated not

"GEOLOGY TO THE LEFT OF US. GEOLOGY TO THE RIGHT OF US. WHEREVER WE LOOK, GEOLOGY. AND WE CAN GET IN ON THE GROUND FLOOR."

by Jules Verne's fictional devices described in the *Voyage to the Center of the Earth,* but by a more powerful tool: the method of science.

There have been many models of the Earth, possibly starting with the idea that the Earth was a flat disk carried on the backs of seven giant turtles on a vast ocean. The turtles did not last long, but the flat shape did. As a result, sailors feared sailing off the edge of the Earth.

Long ago, there were people who believed the Earth was hollow—a thin outer shell and a void in the center. There are still people who believe in this void, except they say creatures from outer space live there. Others have different fears. In the 1960s, the Congress of the United States was considering legislation to finance the drilling of a test well under the ocean in an effort to penetrate the ocean floor and sample the underlying material. Several concerned people wrote letters telling their senators and representatives that if such a hole were bored, it would unplug the stop, so to speak, and all the ocean's water would drain away into the middle of the Earth!

The most recent model—the plate tectonics model—dispenses with the ocean-going turtles, the flat shape, and the void. The following sections will examine five observations on which this model is based, and then two predictions that have tested its validity.

Five Important Earthly Observations

The first observations to be examined concern the portion of the Earth that is most readily accessible—the surface. Admittedly, much of the familiar surface is soil. But, generally speaking, you do not have to dig very far to get down to rock, and it is rock that is most characteristic of the material of the Earth's surface.

One property of rocks, or of any other kind of matter, is that of density. The *density* of any object is the object's *mass* (the amount of material contained in an object) divided by the object's *volume* (the amount of space the object occupies):

$$\text{density} = \frac{\text{mass of object}}{\text{volume of object}}$$

Now suppose you had a whole collection of cubes of the same kind of rock, all of which had the same mass and the same volume. The density of one of these cubes would be determined by dividing the rock cube's mass by its volume:

$$\text{density of 1 cube} = \frac{\text{mass of cube}}{\text{volume of cube}}$$

What would be the density of two rock cubes stuck together? Well, the mass would be doubled, and so would the volume. However, because the cubes are made of the same type of rock, the density would be the same as the density of a single cube:

$$\text{density of 2 cubes} = \frac{2 \times \text{mass of cube}}{2 \times \text{volume of cube}}$$

$$= \text{density of 1 cube}$$

No matter how many cubes are stuck together, as long as all the cubes are made of the same type of rock, the density of the aggregate is identical to that of a single cube. Thus, if the density of a single rock was found and if the whole Earth was made of that same kind of rock, then the whole Earth would have the same density as that single rock.

Now, as any geologist will tell you, there are many varieties of rocks. If the densities of these various rocks are measured, it turns out that almost all the surface rocks are between 2 and 3.5 times the density of water. Thus, if the Earth were made uniformly of these rocks, the average density of the whole Earth should be between 2 and 3.5 times the density of water.

It is not—the Earth's average density is about 5.4 times that of water!

To summarize:

OBSERVATION 1   Surface rocks have densities between 2 and 3.5 times the density of water; the whole Earth has a density 5.4 times that of water. The implication of this observation is that the final hypothesis must take into account the fact that the materials below the surface of the Earth must be more dense than those on the surface.

Another observation involves the Earth's magnetic field. It is the effect of this field that makes the needle of a compass always align on a north-south axis. A study of rocks of various ages from many different areas of the Earth indicates that the Earth's magnetic field has reversed directions many times at irregular intervals. In other words, the north and south poles have switched magnetic orientations.

OBSERVATION 2 The Earth has a magnetic field that has reversed its direction many times during the last few million years. The hypothesis that is finally adopted will have to deal with the fact that the Earth has a magnetic field and provide some possible mechanism for this field's reversal.

Some occasionally devastating phenomena—earthquakes and volcanoes—should also be examined.

OBSERVATION 3 Earthquakes and volcanoes occur primarily within certain geographic zones as shown in Figure 5-1.

The hypothesis will have to explain both the occurrence of earthquakes and volcanoes and the fact that they happen with greater frequency in certain areas.

Now, although the Earth is extremely large and, therefore, difficult to probe, one method of getting below Earth's surface has been developed, a method that uses seismic waves. Seismic waves are profound wavelike movements in the Earth, caused, for example, by earthquakes or the setting off of charges or bombs. Such waves occur in three varieties:

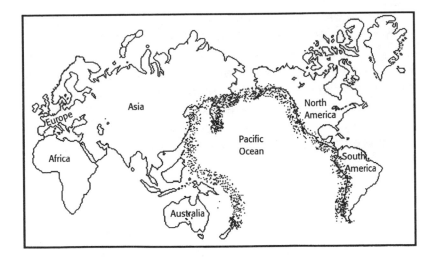

FIGURE 5-1. Earthquake and Volcano Locations (indicated by bands of dots)

P-Waves—Waves that penetrate the Earth's interior and that travel through both solids and liquids; they are reflected and bent as they pass from one kind of solid to another or from solid to liquid.

S-Waves—Waves that penetrate the Earth's interior and that travel through solids only (they are absorbed by liquids); they are reflected and bent as they pass from one kind of solid to another.

L-Waves—Waves that travel only along the Earth's surface.

Seismic waves can be detected by using a seismograph, which consists of a pen rigidly fixed to the rock layer close to the Earth's surface and a paper chart that moves past the pen at a constant rate. Only the pen is free to respond to the Earth's vibration. As the Earth jiggles because of the seismic waves, the pen makes wavy lines on the paper. In remote locations, the pen's jiggles may be broadcast by radio rather than recorded directly on paper. Thousands of seismograph observation stations are located all around the world, and high quality seismic data have been accumulated for quite a long time.

OBSERVATION 4   P- and S-waves are reflected and bent as they travel through the Earth. This suggests the presence of layers of different kinds of solids below the Earth's surface. S-waves are absent in some directions (see Figure 5-2). Because S-waves are absorbed by liquids, their absence indicates the presence of some liquid below the Earth's surface.

OBSERVATION 5   Careful examination of the west coast of Africa and the east coast of South America reveals that the coastlines of these two continents fit together very nicely (see Figure 5.3). When fitted together, regions of fossilized remains as well as mineral deposits on each coast overlap each other.

This close fit led in the 1920s to a hypothesis of continental drift, which suggested that entire continents were capable of movement along the Earth's surface. However,

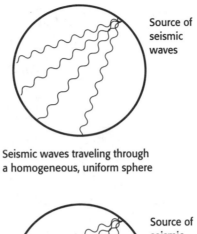

Seismic waves traveling through
a homogeneous, uniform sphere

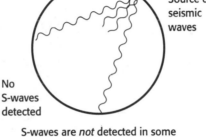

S-waves are *not* detected in some
regions of the Earth.

FIGURE 5-2. Fate of Seismic Waves

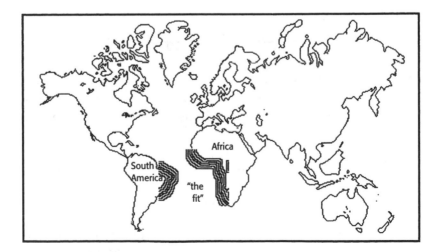

FIGURE 5-3. The Fit between Africa and South America

" I WOULDN'T WORRY. WITH CONTINENTAL DRIFT,
AFRICA OR SOUTH AMERICA SHOULD COME BY
EVENTUALLY. "

no satisfactory mechanism for the cause of the movement
of continents was available at that time.

It All Came Together in 1965

In 1965, geologists were able to propose a hypothesis that
could explain all of these seemingly unrelated observations.
This hypothesis was so comprehensive that it *revolutionized*
the field of geology.

HYPOTHESIS The Plate Tectonics Model of the Earth—
The Earth consists of a sequence of layers, which are, from
the outermost to the innermost:

> *Crust:* A relatively thin, rigid layer; made of fairly low
>   density rock and consisting of a dozen major por-
>   tions and many minor ones.

Mantle: The thickest layer; made of higher density rock that is very hot. At depths below the uppermost mantle, this molten layer flows quite slowly, like a glacier. Currents or local movements within this mantle are caused by hot spots that are the result of uneven cooling and by rotation of the Earth.

Outer Core: A hot liquid that is yet more dense than the mantle. This liquid, which consists mainly of iron and nickel, slowly sloshes around because of the Earth's rotation.

Inner Core: A solid that consists mainly of extremely hot iron. Because it is under intense pressure, it is too dense to remain liquid.

These four layers are shown in Figure 5-4.

The crust plus the uppermost portion of the mantle comprise the *lithosphere,* which is broken into a number of giant mobile slabs or tectonic plates. Movement of these plates relative to one another is made possible because they rest upon softer, weaker mantle material, the *asthenosphere.* Growth and destruction of the plates occurs along their seismically active margins. Although usually slow, plate movement can be quite rapid—in 1905, plates underlying San Francisco moved 20 feet in one minute!

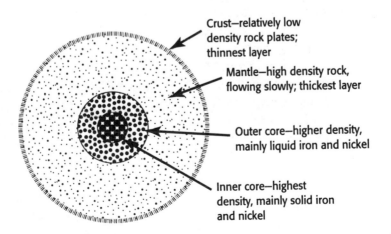

Crust—relatively low density rock plates; thinnest layer

Mantle—high density rock, flowing slowly; thickest layer

Outer core—higher density, mainly liquid iron and nickel

Inner core—highest density, mainly solid iron and nickel

FIGURE 5-4. Model of the Earth

THE MAGIC OF PLATE TECTONICS

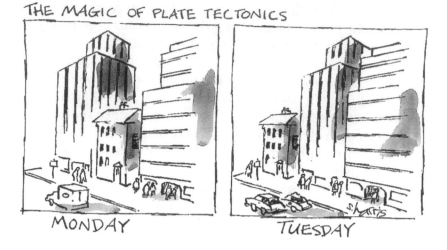

MONDAY   TUESDAY

Here's how the plate tectonics model explains the five observations made earlier.

1. That the material below Earth's surface is of higher density than that on the surface—The mantle and each core are of higher density than the crust.
2. That the Earth has a magnetic field that has reversed direction—Moving charged particles, such as those in liquid iron, are known to generate a magnetic field. The Earth's magnetic field is derived from coordinated movement of these particles in the molten outer core. Reversal of the magnetic field might occur because of changes in the motion of the liquid iron.
3. That earthquakes and volcanoes occur in certain zones—Convection currents in the asthenosphere build up pressures in the plates that make up the lithosphere. These pressures are released by sudden movements of the plates (earthquakes) and by hot molten material (lava) flowing up through the cracks producing giant safety valves called volcanoes. Because almost all of this activity occurs along the cracks, that is where zones of high earthquake and volcano activity are observed.

4. That S-waves are absent in some directions—The liquid outer core absorbs S-waves.
5. That there is continental drift—The plates, or crustal rafts, carrying continents such as South America and Africa drifted apart because currents in the underlying mantle dragged them away from each other.

Plate Tectonics Put to the Test

Continental drift, as shown in Figure 5-5, has taken place over extremely long periods of time. About 200 million years ago, all the continents fitted together to form a super-continent called *Pangea,* or "all land." Pangea floated in a

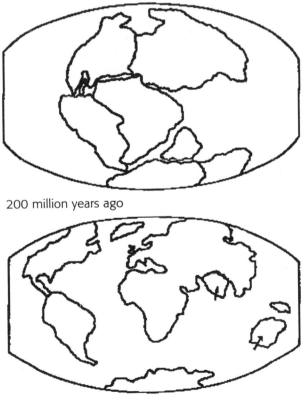

200 million years ago

Today

FIGURE 5-5. Continental Drift

superocean called *Panthalassa,* or "all sea." One striking feature of the breakup of Pangea is the collision between the plate carrying India with the main Eurasian plate. This collision was so intense that it "wrinkled up" the plates along the line of the collision and formed the highest mountains in the world, the Himalayas.

PREDICTION 1 The Earth's plates will continue to move. Movements of several centimeters per year (about as fast as fingernails grow) should be measurable.

EXPERIMENT 1 The movement of these plates relative to each other has been measured in many different locations by very accurate means; the results agree with numerical predictions. An example of this movement is in the state of California, which is located on two different plates. The edges of these plates meet in what is called the San Andreas Fault, and the rather erratic motion of these two plates as their jagged edges occasionally suddenly slide past each other produces the earthquakes that plague the area. Nine moderate-to-severe earthquakes have been accompanied by movements of this fault since 1838.

The second prediction, a rather bold and detailed pre-diction whose confirmation makes the plate tectonics hy-pothesis particularly attractive, deals with another phenome-non that happens when plates drift. In some locations, as two plates move apart, the boundary between the plates is filled in with molten rock. When such spreading occurs beneath the oceans (see Figure 5-6), it is called sea-floor spreading, a "wound that never heals," for the process recurs repeatedly.

The molten rock is initially hot and very dense. As it moves up, the ocean water cools it off, and it solidifies at the bottom of the ocean.

PREDICTION 2   If this material has been boiling up and then solidifying on the ocean floor for a long time, then any natural magnets (magnetic minerals) in this new crustal material should have been able to act like compass needles and align themselves with the Earth's magnetic field at the time the rock was molten, as shown in Figure 5-7.

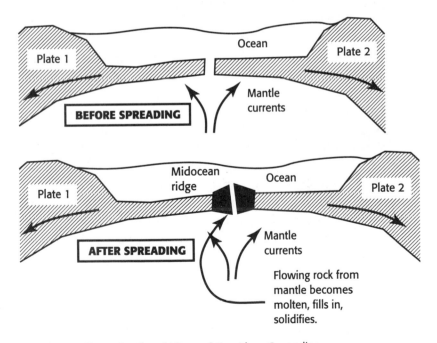

FIGURE 5-6. Cross-Sectional View of Sea-Floor Spreading

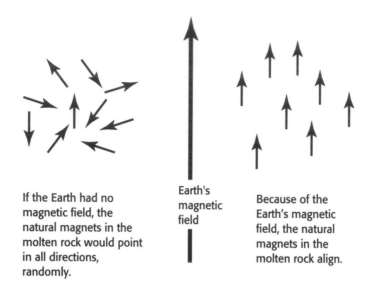

If the Earth had no magnetic field, the natural magnets in the molten rock would point in all directions, randomly.

Earth's magnetic field

Because of the Earth's magnetic field, the natural magnets in the molten rock align.

FIGURE 5-7. Alignment of Natural Magnets in Rocks

When the rock solidified, these natural magnets would then be frozen in this position. Because the Earth's magnetic field has reversed many times, solidified rocks formed during each reversal should provide a permanent record of these events.

EXPERIMENT 2 The predicted pattern was confirmed in 1968 by deep-water drilling projects and magnetic-field mapping, both ship- and airplane-based. Rocks on either side of the spreading center were uniformly older the farther they were from the center. They also showed a symmetric pattern of alternating magnetic polarities on either side of the center. The Earth continues to produce these stripes as if they were on a sea-floor conveyor belt, leaving them as evidence for explorers to find (see Figure 5-8).

The structure of the Earth is somewhat like a partially hardboiled egg with a cracked shell. In a sense, this layered structure fits very nicely with the theory of the Earth's formation—as the materials from a portion of a star's supernova came together, the denser materials sank and the

TOP VIEW OF SPREADING PLATES

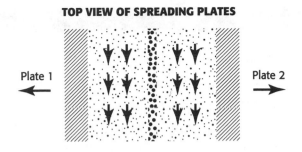

Natural magnets in molten mantle material align with the Earth's magnetic field, then solidify in place.

Time passes;
the Earth's magnetic field reverses.
New material from the mantle oozes up.

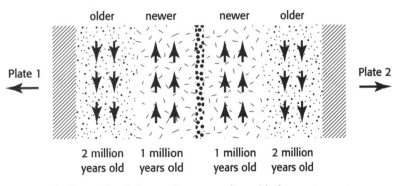

The "newer" rocks' natural magnets align with the most recent direction of the Earth's magnetic field, then solidify into place.

FIGURE 5-8. Predicted and Actual Magnetic-Field Pattern of Sea-Floor Rocks

lighter ones rose, leading to the pattern postulated by the plate tectonics model. Certainly, more will be learned about this planet from deep-drilling projects, continued seismic-wave monitoring, and so on. Curiously, however, some details of the Earth's formation are being provided by exploration of the moon, Mars, Venus, and Jupiter, which are at different stages of development. Sometimes, some perspective can be gained from a distance.

Idea Folders

23 Earthquake Prediction

24 Chaos Theory, Weather Prediction, and the Butterfly Effect

25 Geological Similarities between the Earth and Other Planets

26 Formation of Earth's Moon: The Giant Impact Theory

CHAPTER SIX

Big Idea #5

Biology's Theory of Evolution: Life Begins and Branches Out

The progress of science is strewn, like an ancient desert trail, with the bleached skeletons of discarded theories which once seemed to possess eternal life.

Arthur Koestler

Biology is the study of every kind of living thing on Earth. Because we human beings are a part of this broad spectrum of life forms, we place a premium on human life. We wonder about its nature so that we can sustain and improve it. We seek to unlock nature's secrets, answer such questions as, "How does life arise?"; "How long has it been around?"; "Why does it behave the way it does?" Answers to these questions get at the very nature of the brief existence of human life in this universe. To help understand how we fit into the grand scheme of the universe, we seek to find out how we came to be what we are.

According to the nebular hypothesis, Earth was formed about 5 billion years ago from condensation of the nuclei

"IF WE COULD JUST TAP INTO THE COLLECTIVE UNCONSCIOUS OF THE AMOEBA — THEN WE'D KNOW HOW IT ALL BEGAN."

formed in a star that underwent a supernova many years prior. At the time of this condensation, no life was present on Earth. Today, there is an incredible variety of living things present on this planet. How might this phenomenal change from no life to diverse life have come about?

The Theory of Evolution is biology's answer to this question. It explains how the first simple life form might have originated and how the great variety of life forms might have arisen from an initial life form.

Maggots, Meat, and Microscopes

Aristotle observed that flies and other insects swarmed around decaying material. This led him to believe that some animals come into being not from the union of male and female, but from the decaying material itself. He said these transformations occurred by the "spontaneous action of Nature." This belief persisted into the 1600s. In 1668, Francesco Redi put it to the test.

OBSERVATION   Redi had observed that maggots form when meat is allowed to rot in an uncovered container.

HYPOTHESIS   According to the prevailing theory, maggot development was an example of the *spontaneous generation of complex organisms from simple nonliving material* (the decaying meat).

PREDICTION   This theory predicts that maggots would also develop if the meat was placed in a container that was then covered with a wire gauze. (If the maggots came from the meat itself, the gauze should not make any difference.)

EXPERIMENT   Maggots did *not* develop in the gauze-covered container prepared by Redi.

Redi was able to explain these results by pointing out that flies swarm about rotting meat and deposit eggs that develop into maggots (fly larvae). In the experiment, flies laid their eggs on the gauze and not on the meat.

Because of this experiment and others, biologists eventually became convinced that complex organisms were not generated spontaneously from nonliving matter. Yet, a better theory was not at all obvious. Biologists needed time to improve their powers of observation. The microscope was invented, better dissection techniques were developed, and so on. Biologists were then able to observe much more detail, much more complexity, and much more variety. They came to appreciate that one of the major difficulties with the hypothesis about the spontaneous generation of complex organisms is that it makes a tremendous jump by going directly from simple substances to complex organisms. The difference in complexity level is just too great.

This suggests that the first organism must have been the simplest unit that exhibits the characteristics of life, namely a *cell.* How might the first cell have originated? To answer this question, you need to take a look first at modern-day cells and then at an hypothesis that describes how similar structures might have been generated a long time ago.

A Quick Tour of the Cell

With the development of sophisticated instruments for examining cells, tremendous advances have been made in understanding the details of the nature of cells. Techniques for staining portions of the cell and the use of powerful (electron) microscopes have provided a clear picture of cell structure. The basic parts of an animal cell, as shown in Figure 6-1, are a *nucleus,* which contains stringy structures called *chromosomes;* the *cytoplasm,* which forms the vast majority of the cell outside of the nucleus; and the *cell membrane,* which surrounds the cytoplasm.

In contrast to animal cells, plant cells are surrounded by walls.

For the cell structure to exist, three basic requirements must be met: (1) a plan or blueprint (2) building materials,

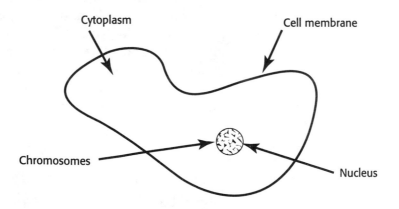

FIGURE 6-1. Simplified Diagram of an Animal Cell

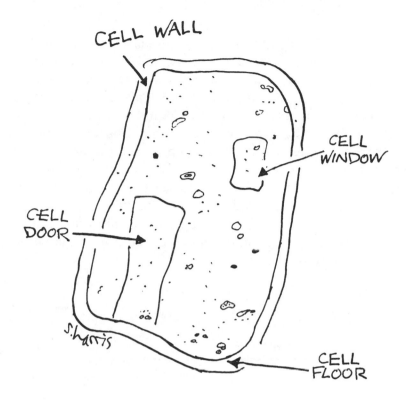

and (3) a means of carrying out or facilitating the translation of the plan.

What's in Charge Here?

Biologists sought the master planner of the cell for a long time. They observed that removal of the nucleus from the cytoplasm of an amoeba cell causes it to die. On the other hand, the nucleus by itself could not sustain life. They hypothesized that the nucleus is the master planner; the nucleus needs the cytoplasm (to control) and the cytoplasm needs the nucleus (to control it). But wait a minute! Could it be that the cytoplasm needs the nucleus (to control) and the nucleus needs the cytoplasm (to control it)? Why not hypothesize that the cytoplasm is the master planner?

To determine what is in charge, a relatively simple experiment was carried out on a single-celled *alga,* which is a plant lacking true stems, roots, and leaves. Individuals of this plant consist of a base that contains its nucleus, a stalk (cytoplasm), and a cap. Two species were used: one with a flat cap, the other with a lobed cap. When the cap of each was cut off, each regrew its own kind of cap (see Figure 6-2).

If the hypothesis that the nucleus is the master planner were correct, one could predict that if the caps were removed and the stalk of each was grafted onto the nucleus-containing base of the other, the caps that grew back would correspond to the original base.

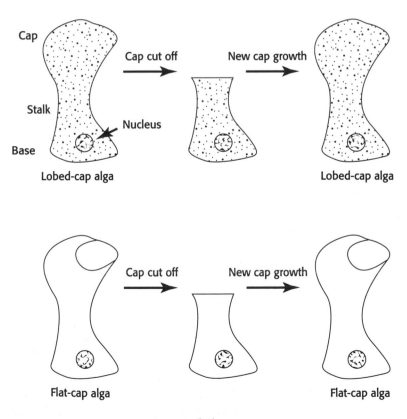

FIGURE 6-2. Regeneration of Caps of Algae

When the experiment was performed, as shown in Figure 6-3, the cap that grew back initially corresponded to the stalk, not the base. However, if the newly grown cap was cut off, the next cap grown matched the base, not the stalk. Subsequent decapitations also resulted in caps that matched the base.

The appearance of the first regenerated cap can be explained by the retention in the stalk of some regenerative substance created by the original nucleus. By the time the second cap was formed, this substance was used up and the stalk had to rely on the substance created by its new nucleus to produce the new cap. Thus, the cell's plan is contained in the nucleus.

But where in the nucleus is the plan located? To answer this question, in 1928, experiments were performed with two strains of bacteria, R-type and S-type. The S-type bacteria grew a structure called a *capsule* (gelatinous coat) and also gave laboratory mice pneumonia; the R-type did not grow a capsule and did not give laboratory mice pneumonia. Heat-killed, S-type bacteria could not cause pneumonia in mice. However, a mixture of dead S-type and live R-type bacteria resulted in capsule growth in the R-type bacteria, and this mixture did cause pneumonia in mice. It seemed that something in the dead S-type bacteria had caused the R-type bacteria to grow capsules and exhibit S-like behavior. Which component within the dead S-type bacteria caused this transformation?

In 1944, the dead S-type bacteria were separated by extraction into their components, and each component was paired with live R-type to see which would cause the development of S-like behavior. The component responsible for the transformation was found to be the one in extract 44, but its composition could not be analyzed at that time. Extract 44 was identified in 1953 as the highly complex, giant molecules called *deoxyribonucleic* (*nucleic* = found in the nucleus) *acid,* DNA for short. Thus, with excellent hindsight, 25 years of difficult experimental work can be fit into the scientific method sequence:

OBSERVATION R-type and S-type bacteria differ only in that S-type contain a capsule and cause pneumonia in

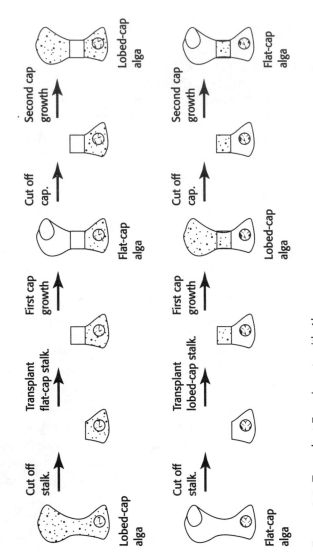

Figure 6-3. Transplant Experiments with Algae

laboratory mice, whereas R-type do not contain a capsule and do not cause pneumonia in laboratory mice.

HYPOTHESIS DNA can control the structural and functional characteristics of cells.

PREDICTION DNA from dead S-type bacteria, when mixed with and absorbed by live R-type, will cause R-type to become S-like, that is, to grow capsules and cause pneumonia in laboratory mice.

EXPERIMENT A mixture of DNA from dead S-type bacteria and live R-type does cause pneumonia in laboratory mice. The fact that DNA from S-type bacteria causes the transformation of R-type bacteria supports the hypothesis. This, along with other experimental evidence, confirms the role of DNA as the key to cell growth and function.

The Message and the Messenger

DNA is the major constituent of the chromosomes, which are located in the nucleus. If DNA is found only in the nucleus, how does its plan get communicated to the cytoplasm? How is DNA able to control the building process that takes place in the cytoplasm? DNA's plan is communicated by a substance that is found in the nucleus *and* in the cytoplasm: *ribonucleic acid,* or RNA. DNA builds the RNA molecule, which moves into the cytoplasm as a kind of messenger. The RNA has transcribed some of the information encoded in the DNA (the genetic code) and carries it to the cytoplasm. (It was RNA in the transplanted alga stalk that was the regenerative substance that determined the structure of the first cap regenerated.) There, molecules called enzymes are built. *Enzymes* act as *catalysts*—substances that do not participate in a chemical reaction themselves but allow the reaction to proceed at a faster rate and at a lower temperature. In turn, these enzymes control the chemical reactions that determine cell structure and functions and, ultimately, the traits of the organism.

Message, Messenger, and Materials

Cell traits are determined by the DNA of the cell. Information about these traits gets into the cytoplasm via RNA. The RNA helps build the enzymes that in turn determine how the available building materials are assembled within the cells. Building materials are available in the form of a wide variety of molecules or nutrients that can be combined to form other molecules. The overall process is illustrated in Figure 6-4.

The three things required for a modern cell to exist have been identified: (1) the plan—the DNA molecule; (2) the building materials—nutrient molecules; and (3) the means of carrying out or facilitating the translation of the plan—RNA and enzyme molecules. DNA, RNA, enzymes, and the building materials and what the cell makes from them are all *molecules*—they are collections of atoms that have been altered in some way to form stable groupings. Thus, in the final analysis, there is a *molecular basis* for the structure and functioning of the cell—and, therefore, the possibility of a *molecular basis* for the genesis of the first cell.

Although that first cell need not have been as intricate as modern cells, it should have contained a planning molecule capable of replication, plus the nutrient molecules from which other cell components could be built.

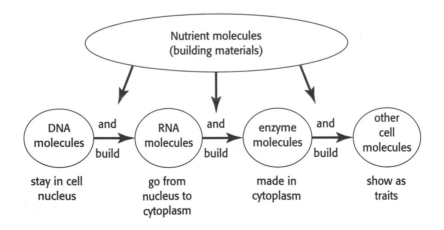

FIGURE 6-4. Cell Growth and Function

How might such cell components have come into being? How might the chemical reactions leading to their formation have occurred? For any chemical reaction to occur, the appropriate ingredients and conditions must be available. The ingredients, the major atoms from which the cell components are built, are carbon (C), oxygen (O), hydrogen (H), and nitrogen (N). Thus, to construct these cell components, appropriate molecules containing these four atoms must be available.

From Molecules to Cells

One hypothesis that has been proposed is that, around 4.5 billion years ago, the surface of the Earth was covered largely by water (H_2O) and surrounded by an atmosphere composed of ammonia (NH_3), methane (CH_4), and hydrogen (H_2), with no free oxygen (O_2) or ozone (O_3) present. This atmosphere did not filter out the sun's high-energy radiation, and so this radiation plus lightning from violent storms in the atmosphere could help generate a series of

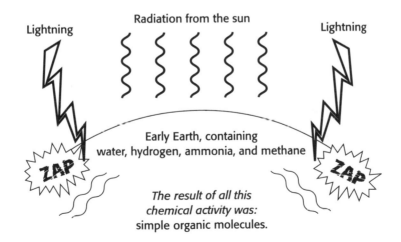

FIGURE 6-5. The Early Earth Synthesizing Simple Organic Molecules

chemical reactions (see Figure 6-5). These reactions in turn could have produced a sequence of increasingly complex organic molecules that contained carbon atoms linked together. These molecules might have accumulated in the warm soup of the surface water.

Simple organic molecules could then have combined, giving rise to the larger, more complex molecules that abound in cells today. Some of these could have been enzymes, others were possibly able to condense into membranes to contain the cell. Eventually, possibly 4 billion years ago, membrane-bounded cells, or bags of active molecules, came into being. From the soup of the seas, a type of molecular evolution was occurring, eventually producing the first primitive cell, as shown in Figure 6-6.

Even though genetic information usually flows from DNA to RNA today, many investigators think that some form of RNA was the initial planning molecule and that this RNA made possible the evolution of DNA. The RNA molecule was somehow able to organize some of the material in the soup to form cell substances, including new RNA molecules. In a sense, the soup was nourishing itself! Life, in this sense, can be defined as *a behavior pattern that chemical systems exhibit when they reach a certain kind and level of complexity*.

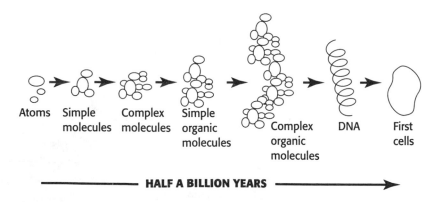

Atoms　Simple　Complex　Simple　　　Complex　DNA　First
　　　molecules　molecules　organic　　organic　　　cells
　　　　　　　　　　molecules　　molecules

◀────────── HALF A BILLION YEARS ──────────▶

FIGURE 6-6. Spontaneous Molecular Generation of the First Cell

Miller Supports Oparin

In 1936, the Russian biochemist Alexander I. Oparin formulated a hypothesis about the origin of life—this hypothesis can be called the spontaneous molecular generation of the first cell (in contrast to Aristotle's spontaneous generation of complex organisms).

HYPOTHESIS Under the conditions of the Earth's early atmosphere, available molecules participated in a chain of molecular reactions that ultimately produced living cells.

PREDICTION If the ingredients and conditions of the early atmosphere could be duplicated in the laboratory, the hypothesized chain of molecular events could occur, ultimately producing a living cell from simple molecules.

EXPERIMENT In 1953, Stanley Miller tried to replicate what was then believed to be the chemistry of the prebiotic Earth. He mixed water and an atmosphere of ammonia, methane, and hydrogen in a glass tube. He then subjected these molecules to a continuous high-energy electrical current, similar to the lightning that might have ripped through the Earth's early atmosphere (see Figure 6-7). The experiment produced a variety of organic molecules of the kind found in cells, but not one living cell.

Although Miller's experiment showed that essentially random chemistry could yield biological substances and provided some support for Oparin's hypothesis, the experiment did not address many other links in the chain leading to the formulation of life itself. This feat has not been demonstrated in the laboratory. Even if life was created in the laboratory, it would not provide complete support for Oparin's hypothesis, which says that it *did* happen that way. Whatever occurred did so at a time when no witnesses were present.

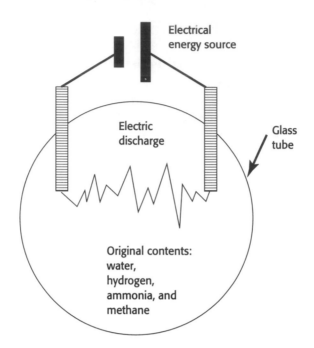

Figure 6-7. Miller's Apparatus for Synthesizing Simple Organic Molecules from Simpler Molecules

Atmospheric Evolution

Of the four ingredients in the Miller experiment, only one—water vapor—exists in significant amounts in the atmosphere today. The modern atmosphere is almost totally nitrogen (N_2) and oxygen. This change in the composition of the atmosphere was a result of the development of living things.

Early cells used molecules from the sea as their source of food and energy. It is believed that the cell population grew rapidly and the supply of necessary nutrients began to run out. The soup was eating itself into oblivion! (Was this the first ecological crisis?) Later, other cells developed that used colored compounds (pigments such as chlorophyll *a*) to absorb visible light energy. This was a revolutionary step because, previously, only ultraviolet light, absorbed during the formation of molecules in the sea, was utilized for energy input. These new cells used water, carbon dioxide (CO_2), and energy directly from the sun to produce energy-rich molecules. This process is called *photosynthesis* and produces oxygen as a by-product:

Lower energy molecules ($CO_2 + H_2O$)	+	Energy from the sun (in the presence of chlorophyll *a*)	→	Higher energy organic molecules	+	Oxygen (O_2)

High in the atmosphere, oxygen molecules are converted to ozone, which acts as a shield, cutting down the amount of ultraviolet radiation reaching the Earth's surface.

Atmospheric conditions have changed drastically during the past 4 billion years. In addition to the oxygen produced by photosynthesis, there is elemental nitrogen produced by the action of certain bacteria on nitrogen compounds. As a result, molecular generation of cells cannot be expected to occur today in the way Oparin's hypothesis indicates. Yet, the current atmosphere and surroundings do allow the development of variety in the biosphere.

Life Branches Out

According to Oparin's hypothesis, the first simple cell, the first life form, emerged around 4 billion years ago. How can that hypothesis be extended to explain the incredible variety of life forms that exist on Earth today?

An answer to this question was published in 1859 by Charles Darwin, an English naturalist, in *On the Origin of Species*. Darwin wrote:

As many more individuals are produced than can possibly survive, there must in every case be a struggle for existence, either one individual with another of the same species, or with the individuals of distinct species, or with the physical conditions of life. . . . Can it, then, be thought improbable, seeing that variations useful to man have undoubtedly occurred, that other variations useful in some way to each being in the great and complex battle of life, should sometimes occur in the course of thousands of generations? If such do occur, can we doubt (remembering that many more individuals are born than can possible survive) that individuals having any advantage, however slight, over others, would have the best chance of surviving and of procreating their kind? On the other hand, we may feel sure that any variation in the least degree injurious would be rigidly destroyed. This preservation of favourable variations and the rejection of injurious variations, I call Natural Selection.

When Darwin presented his theory of natural selection, he was sure that some sort of hereditary mechanism existed to explain the variations, but its nature was unknown. The discrete units of heredity, called *genes,* were first identified by the Augustinian monk Gregor Mendel in Darwin's lifetime but did not become widely known until the twentieth century. Eventual fusion of Darwin's notion of fluctuations in hereditary material and Mendel's concept of genetic variation is often referred to as neo-Darwinism, or the modern synthesis.

Over the past 40 years, yet another synthesis has occurred, one that encompasses an understanding of evolutionary processes at the molecular level. *Molecular biology,* the study of biology from a molecular perspective, has advanced enormously the knowledge of biological evolution. Mendel's genes are now known to be segments of DNA molecules. Because molecular biology provides the most detailed evidence of evolutionary changes, this discussion will focus on the modern view of evolution: change in the genetic composition of a population through time.

All life forms contain DNA. Their structures are determined by the specific kind of DNA they contain. How can DNA molecules change, becoming more complex and varied, leading to more complex organisms and a variety of different organisms? To answer that question, it is necessary to investigate the circumstances that affect such changes and the way that the altered DNA can be used to produce new organisms.

Multiplication by Division

New organisms are generated by asexual and sexual reproduction. In *asexual reproduction, a cell* produces a copy of itself through a complex process called *mitosis.* What is the fate of the DNA molecules in the chromosomes during mitosis?

Different organisms have different numbers of chromosomes in their cells; for example, each cell of a normal human being (except the sex cell) contains 46 chromosomes in 23 pairs, as shown in Figure 6-8.

During mitosis, the DNA molecules of each chromosome of the original cell are duplicated. This doubled number of chromosomes then divides evenly, producing two identical cells. When a cell within a human being's body

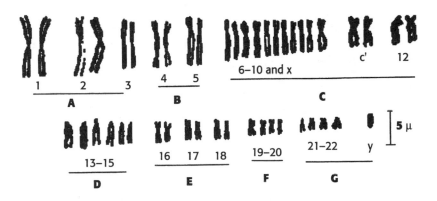

FIGURE 6-8. Chromosomes of a Human Male, Arranged in Decreasing Order of Length and Numbered Accordingly

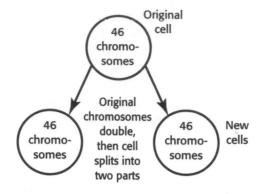

FIGURE 6-9. Results of Mitosis in Humans

reproduces by mitosis, 46 chromosomes double, and the cell then splits into two parts (see Figure 6-9).

In addition to being a process for the reproduction of cells in a multicellular organism, mitosis is also the means of reproduction of simple yet complete organisms like amoebas.

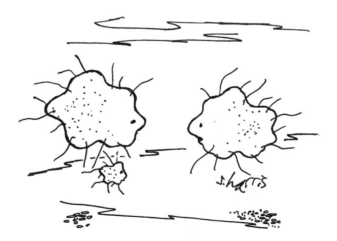

"HE LOOKS JUST LIKE YOU, BUT HE LOOKS JUST LIKE ME, TOO."

Cell variety in multicellular organisms can be explained by *differentiation*, in which portions of the DNA collection are turned on or off at different stages in the growth process. Differentiation results in specialized cells that perform unique functions. Thus, although all your cells contain the same set of 46 chromosomes (except for sex cells, which contain 23 chromosomes), only certain parts of the chromosomes are active in a particular cell dictating that a new cell produced by mitosis be, for example, a skin cell or a brain cell. One complete set of chromosomes acts like the complete set of plans for a large and complicated building. Although all the construction supervisors have complete sets of plans, each supervisor refers only to that portion of the plans that pertains to a specific part of the building.

Multiplication by Addition

Many living things reproduce by a process called *sexual reproduction.* In this process a cell from the male and a cell from the female unite, leading ultimately to the formation of a new individual having genetic material donated by both parents. If each parent contributed its full complement of genetic material, the offspring's cells would have twice as much genetic material as either parent. This is not the case. Rather, through a process called *meiosis,* the collection of chromosomes doubles and then divides into four parts, forming sex cells, which have half the number of chromosomes of their parent cells. As shown in Figure 6-10, the resulting sex cells from each parent then unite to produce a fertilized egg containing a full complement of chromosomes. This fertilized egg then develops into a complete organism by the process of mitosis.

Although the sets of chromosomes contributed by each parent are identical in type and number of chromosomes, they differ in the specific information they contain. This means that organisms that reproduce sexually have a built-in mechanism for generating variety: The two different sets

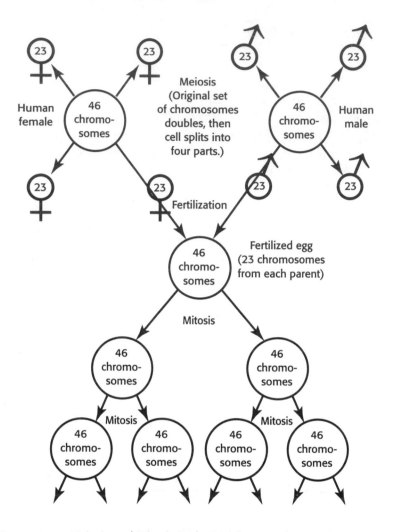

FIGURE 6-10. Meiosis and Mitosis Both Contribute to the Development of the Human Organism

combine to form a unique new set. Furthermore, because each chromosome in the cell that produced sex cells is different, when the chromosome collection is divided, each of the sex cells will contain a unique collection of chromosomes. As a result, succeeding offspring produced by the same set of parents will also be unique.

Nobody's Perfect

DNA of one generation is linked to the DNA of the next generation in either form of reproduction. Thus, changes in the DNA molecules involved in reproduction can cause changes in succeeding generations of the organism involved. Changes in the DNA molecules are referred to as *mutations.* Mutations produce variety, but what produces mutations?

The largest number of mutations occur when DNA molecules are copied during the mitosis process. This is called *random copy error.* On a purely chance or random basis, the subunits that compose the DNA molecule combine in an order other than the original one, thus producing a mutation. These mutations occur naturally and constantly at a low frequency. Other mutations can be caused by: some viral diseases that attack and alter genetic material; high-energy particles (for example, cosmic rays) that rip right through the complex structures, causing changes along their path; certain drugs (such as thalidomide) that interfere with and alter DNA's normal functioning; and high-energy radiation (X rays and gamma rays), which weakens bonds between atoms in molecules and, thereby, can alter their structure. In organisms that reproduce by sexual reproduction, there are additional mechanisms for introducing variety. During meiosis, chromosomes might exchange segments, resulting in new arrangements within chromosome collections.

Random Mutation + Natural Selection = Biological Evolution

Mutations occurring over a 4-billion-year period had the potential to create an enormous variety of life forms. Figure 6-11 shows a segment of this potential "tree of life."

The *full* potential of the mutated variants is not realized in nature, however, for there are many factors that

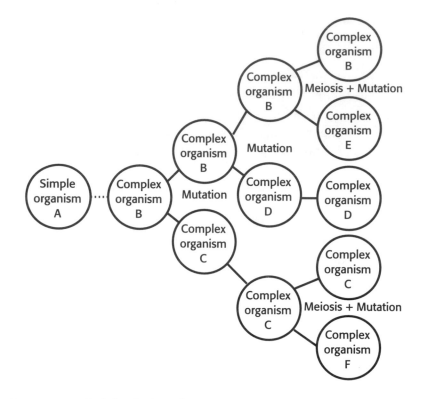

FIGURE 6-11. Variation in Organisms Due to Mutations

limit the perpetuation of variety. The key questions here are: (1) Does a mutant organism actually produce a new generation that carries unique DNA molecules? and (2) Will the offspring survive long enough to reproduce? These questions can be answered in the form of a hypothesis.

HYPOTHESIS   The present variety of life forms can be explained by a two-step process: *random mutation,* in which mutations occur randomly, making possible a large variety of organisms; and *natural selection,* in which the organisms that survive are the ones that can and do reproduce successfully, thereby passing on their genetic material to a next generation.

Random mutation is *inevitable* because mutation is a natural phenomenon. Selection is *inevitable* because almost any natural population of organisms produces more offspring than can be supported by the limited supply of natural resources. Those organisms whose characteristics (genetic variants) have best equipped them to compete for this supply survive and reproduce. For example, naturally occurring geologic changes, such as glacier movements, produce changes in climate that may cause extinctions of entire species if the population lacks variants capable of reproducing under the changed conditions. In this manner, certain variations that arise randomly each generation become predominant.

Because DNA is the key to mutations, the selection process can be diagramed in terms of the DNA molecules of organisms (see Figure 6-12).

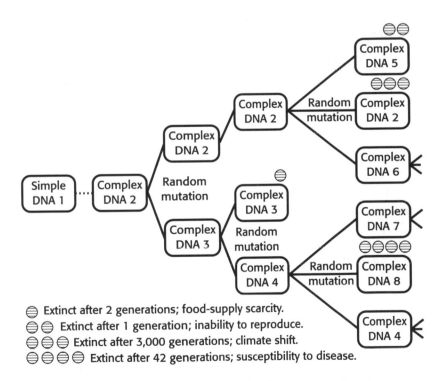

Extinct after 2 generations; food-supply scarcity.
Extinct after 1 generation; inability to reproduce.
Extinct after 3,000 generations; climate shift.
Extinct after 42 generations; susceptibility to disease.

FIGURE 6-12. Schematic of Random Mutation/Natural Selection Process

The tree of life in Figure 6-12 indicates that all living organisms have common ancestors. The details of this hypothesis are impossible to fill in because of the extremely long time intervals involved, and because of the large numbers of mutant forms and extinctions that occurred without leaving traces. What would be ideal would be to have samples of the DNA of all past living things so that the way the DNA evolved over time could be studied. Of course, a complete DNA collection is not obtainable, but archaeologists and biologists search on for scraps of evidence about significant missing links in the evolutionary chain, especially that branch leading to human beings.

Biological Evolution Put to the Test

Two prediction/experimentation sequences based on the random mutation/natural selection hypothesis can be examined.

PREDICTION 1　In a normal bacteria colony, random mutations produce varieties that happen to be resistant to the drug penicillin. In a penicillin-free environment, these penicillin-resistant bacteria have no special advantage over any other bacteria; hence, they constitute a small fraction of the total colony. If penicillin is introduced into the colony, the mutants resistant to penicillin should survive, and the others should die. The penicillin will act as a selecting agent, deciding which bacteria survive. As a result, a colony of penicillin-resistant bacteria should evolve.

EXPERIMENT 1　Penicillin-resistant bacteria colonies have been generated in laboratory experiments after penicillin is introduced into the colony.

PREDICTION 2　Although most kinds of mosquitos can be killed by DDT, some mutant mosquitos happen to be resistant to DDT. If enough of these mutants exist in a particular group, a new group composed of DDT-immune mosquitos will predominate after the original group is sprayed with DDT.

EXPERIMENT 2   Mosquito groups in many areas of the world are now resistant to DDT.

Regardless of these and other supporting prediction/ experiment sequences, the question about the overall hypothesis still remains: Was this the way this phenomenon *did* occur? The method of science cannot answer this question because whatever occurred happened when no witnesses were available. Still, science can hypothesize about ways it might have happened and accept the simplest hypothesis that generates predictions supported by experimental evidence. These are the rules by which the game of science is played.

Spontaneous Generation Updated

Aristotle believed that decaying material could be transformed by the "spontaneous action of Nature" into living animals. His hypothesis was ultimately rejected, but, in a way, he might not have been completely wrong. Aristotle's hypothesis has been replaced by *another* spontaneous generation hypothesis, one that requires billions of years to go from the molecules of the universe to cells, and then, via random mutation/natural selection, from cells to the variety of organisms living today. This version, which postulates chance happenings eventually leading to the phenomenon of life, is biology's Theory of Evolution. The overall sequence is illustrated in Figure 6-13.

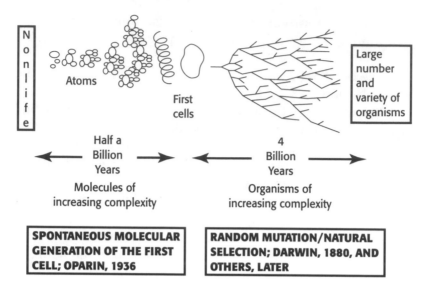

FIGURE 6-13. From Nonlife to Life: The Path of Increasing Complexity

Idea Folders

27 The Lock-and-Key Theory of Enzymes

28 A Biology-Geology Linkage

29 The Order in Which Life Developed

30 Viruses: Dead or Alive?

31 The Human Genome Project

32 Potentially Dangerous Knowledge

33 Recombinant Engineering: Pandora's Box?

34 Cloning: Carbon Copies

35 Extraterrestrial Life

CHAPTER SEVEN

The Method of Science

Further Insights

No amount of experimentation can ever prove me right: A single experiment can prove me wrong.

Albert Einstein

Now that the five biggest ideas of science have been set forth, they can be used as examples to gain further insights into how these as well as other scientific ideas are evaluated. The nature of observations, hypotheses, predictions, and experiments will be reexamined, as will the reasoning processes that are used to proceed from one stage to the next.

Observation versus Experimentation

Observation and experimentation are the "facts" upon which scientific hypotheses are based. Although observation precedes hypothesis formation and experimentation follows prediction, when a hypothesis needs to be recycled, the experiments are included as observations leading to the recycled hypothesis.

Both observation and experimentation demand valid, specific measurements of physical reality. These measurements should be capable of being reproduced by any suitably trained experimenter. For example, accurate determinations of the densities of Earth's surface rocks and of the intensity of the background radiation permeating the universe were needed to support hypotheses about the composition of the Earth and the origin of the universe.

From Observation to Hypothesis

The step from the observations to the hypothesis involves a representation of physical reality by symbols such as letters, numbers, or words, as shown in Figure 7-1. For exam-

"SURE, WE'RE DEALING WITH TINY PARTICLES, BUT YOUR FORMULA IS JUST A SYMBOLIC REPRESENTATION."

ple, the word *planet* in the nebular hypothesis is not itself a "planet"; it just represents one; in formulas, the letter *E* could stand for *energy*.

Belgian surrealist René Magritte made this point with a work of art titled *"Ceci n'est pas une pipe"* ("This is not a pipe"). A purpose of this work was to make people aware that an image or model is not to be confused with the real thing it represents; "being" and "representing" are not the same. (Magritte's work is a kind of analytical cartoon, to which Charlie Wynn has added a line. . . . Okay, from now on we'll leave the cartooning to Sidney!)

The substitution of symbols (such as the word *electron*) for physical reality is referred to as *abstraction*. An example of abstraction is Bohr's making the step from the observable

reality of light emitted by excited atoms to the notion of electrons in separate, distinct energy levels.

Hypothesis formation often requires the creation of a *general* statement about a set of *specific* facts. This kind of reasoning, which proceeds from certain truths to an uncertain generality, is called *inductive reasoning.* In a broader sense, inductive reasoning involved in the formulation of a hypothesis uses a set of observations as premises to *support,* but not to *guarantee,* the truth of the hypothesis. For example, suppose you saw 400 cars on a particular day, and all 400 had four wheels. You could conclude *tentatively* that *all* cars have four wheels. One *infers* from what the observations *imply.* Such reasoning can be misleading—cars with three wheels have been built.

Here is an inductive-reasoning example from chemistry: All of the atoms of chlorine that chemists have tested exhibit certain chemical properties—they react with sodium to form a salt, tend to combine in pairs to form a gaseous substance, and so on. Based on these data, chemists presume that all atoms of chlorine in the entire universe have these same properties. Is that a safe presumption? Chemists have tested only an extremely small fraction of the chlorine atoms on Earth, and yet they are willing to generalize to the entire universe!

Here's a reasoning example from everyday life: You often have crossed a street at an intersection where there is a traffic light and never have observed any cars fail to halt when the light is red. One day, you make an inductive leap and predict that no car will ever run that traffic light. You

OBSERVATION: Sense specific physical realities or events.

Inductive reasoning   Abstraction

HYPOTHESIS: Create a statement about the general nature of the phenomenon observed.

FIGURE 7-1. From Observation to Hypothesis Formation

fearlessly proceed to cross the street. Probability is on your side, but the results could be fatal!

Representing Reality

Hypotheses are usually expressed in words and numbers, symbols that stand for physical realities. For example, the Big Bang hypothesis, stated in words, says: "About 15 billion years ago, all the matter and energy in the universe was concentrated into a single lump, referred to as the primeval fireball. This fireball consisted of. . . ."

Hypotheses can take the form of quantitative relationships, such as the following example involving the radiation given off by excited atoms: One property of radiation is called its *frequency*—the number of complete waves of light that pass a given point in a second. Bohr's hypothesis says that when an electron in an excited atom jumps downward in energy level, the frequency of light given off is related to the difference in energy levels in such a way that the *wider* the energy gap jumped, the *higher* the frequency of light given off.

Relationships of this type are so common in the sciences that a shorthand for expressing them has been developed: mathematics. In this shorthand:

$$\Delta E = hf$$

where ΔE = energy gap (Δ stands for "change in," and E stands for energy)

h = a proportionality constant (number that ties the energy gap and the frequency into an exact relationship or equation)

f = frequency of radiation given off

Mathematics is a kind of language, an almost universal one at that. Because languages are necessary for the communication of hypotheses, mathematics is extremely useful to science. Mathematics, however, is basically a language dealing in relationships among symbols and is, thus, *not* a science, for sciences begin and end with physical reality. Mathematics can explore the possible relationships among abstractions without concern for whether those abstractions have counterparts in the real world.

The physicist C. N. Yang tells a story to illustrate this difference between mathematics and science:

> A man carrying a bundle of clothes was walking down the street when he saw a sign in a shop window: Clothes Washed, 50¢/bundle. The man walked in and asked how long it would take to wash his bundle of clothes. The clerk answered: "We don't wash clothes here." The man protested and pointed to the sign in the window. The clerk said: "Oh, yes. We don't wash clothes. We paint signs."

For a mathematical system, the real world need not matter (although it usually does).

Hypotheses versus Laws versus Theories versus Models

The term *hypothesis* often implies insufficient evidence to provide more than a tentative statement. After a large amount of data has been collected, it might be possible to summarize the information in a more concise way. The result is a *law*—a verbal or mathematical statement of a relationship between phenomena (e.g., the periodic law of the elements or the equation $\Delta E = hf$).

Underlying causes of the law's regularities can sometimes be explained by a theory (e.g., the relationship $\Delta E = hf$ can be explained in terms of the theory that there are distinct energy levels for electrons in atoms).

Theory development can also occur on its own, as an explanation derived directly from observations. This was the case in the theory of evolution. Thus, theories can be unifying principles that explain a body of facts and/or laws that are based on those facts. Sometimes, theories take the form of *models*—representations of reality created to account for phenomena (for example, the quantum mechanical model of the atom).

From Hypothesis to Prediction

Mathematics provides an extremely valuable service to science—a way to make predictions based on hypotheses. Look again at the example of the energy levels in the atom. If the law to be tested is $\Delta E = hf$, you might ask what frequency of light, f, would be predicted if it is known that the energy gap, ΔE, is 6 energy units and the value of h is 2 energy units/frequency unit. It does not take much mathematical experience to figure out that the prediction for this case is that f would be 3 frequency units (6 energy units = 2 energy units/frequency unit × 3 frequency units). Even though this example is grossly oversimplified, it illustrates two important points:

1. The step from hypothesis to prediction involves going from the *general* to the *specific*. In the example given, that meant going from a general symbol Δ*E* to the specific case involving 6 energy units and from the general symbol *f* to 3 frequency units.
2. Mathematically expressed hypotheses can be manipulated and rearranged to make predictions. In the example, the expected frequency of radiated light was calculated, but the hypothesis contained the frequency multiplied by something else. The equation had to be solved to get the frequency all by itself.

The hypotheses of science often become extremely complicated mathematically, involving numerous and lengthy equations and operations, perhaps even requiring the services of a computer. Mathematics studies the way symbolic relationships can be formulated and manipulated. A key contribution of mathematics is that its manipulations allow whatever validity is in the hypothesis to be transferred to the prediction.

This form of logic in which specific truths are derived from general truths is referred to as *deductive reasoning* and is built into the manipulations of mathematics. Here is a simple example: For all fingers (f) and normal hands (h), the total number of fingers is 5 times the number of hands. This can be expressed symbolically:

$$f = h \times 5 \text{ (general relationship)}$$

There are two hands, $h = 2$. (specific instance)

$$f = 2 \times 5 = 10 \text{ (specific conclusion)}$$

Another example can be given in words:

All radiating stars have nuclear fusion going on inside. (general relationship)

The sun is a radiating star. (specific instance)
Therefore, the sun has nuclear fusion going on inside.
   (specific conclusion)

Deductive reasoning takes the initial general statement at face value. A false general statement can lead to a
false conclusion:

All oranges are purple.
You have an orange in your refrigerator.
Your orange is purple!

Deductive reasoning is an absolute necessity in going
from the hypothesis to the prediction. It assures that the
prediction will accurately carry the truth (or falsity) of the
hypothesis to the ultimate test, the experiment. This sequence is shown in Figure 7-2.

From Prediction to Experimentation

The *statement* of the prediction consists of words or numbers; thus, it is symbolic, as is the hypothesis. These words
or numbers are *specific* symbols, as opposed to the *general*
symbols contained in the hypothesis. Because deductive
reasoning is used in arriving at the prediction, the prediction is as valid as the hypothesis.

HYPOTHESIS: Create a statement about the general nature
of the phenomenon observed.

Deductive
reasoning

PREDICTION: Forecast a future occurrence, consistent with
the hypothesis.

FIGURE 7-2. Hypothesis Formation to Prediction

PREDICTION: Forecast a future occurrence, consistent with
　　　　　　　the hypothesis.

　　　　　　　　　　　　　　　　Deabstraction

EXPERIMENT: Carry out a test to see if predicted event occurs.

FIGURE 7-3. Prediction to Experimentation

The step from prediction to experiment shown in Figure 7-3 involves a return to physical reality from the symbolic world of the hypothesis and prediction, a process known as *deabstraction*. Real, measurable physical quantities associated with the symbols must be specified. For example, if it is predicted that f equals 3 frequency units, the meaning of *frequency* must be understood by the experimenter, and some way must be devised to carry out this measurement. Quite a lot of talent might be required to figure out what the theorists mean and how the experimentalists can go about making measurements reliably, completely, and accurately.

Recycling (Once More)

If the prediction is not supported by the experiment, it is clear that the hypothesis must be modified. Modification of hypotheses that have not been supported by experimental evidence calls for plenty of judgment. Should the old hypothesis simply be modified slightly to accommodate the new experimental results, or is it time for an entirely new hypothesis?

If the prediction is supported by the experiment, the game is not over. After all, the prediction and experiment are only specific instances, while the hypothesis is general.

"IT MAY VERY WELL BRING ABOUT IMMORTALITY, BUT IT WILL TAKE FOREVER TO TEST IT."

Thus, each successful experiment is only a partial support of the hypothesis. Even if a scientist happens to discover a hypothesis that is absolutely true, there is no way of knowing that he or she has done so!

Every scientific belief is tentative by its very nature; *every* judgment in science stands on the edge of error and is subject to continual revision and refinement. It is, therefore, dangerous to become too attached to a theory. Scientists must be prepared for and open to surprises.

As shown in Figure 7-4, science is indeed a *never-ending* search for answers.

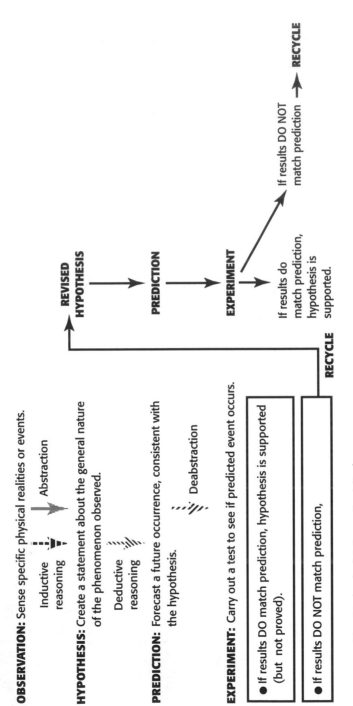

OBSERVATION: Sense specific physical realities or events.

Inductive reasoning

Abstraction

HYPOTHESIS: Create a statement about the general nature of the phenomenon observed.

Deductive reasoning

Deabstraction

PREDICTION: Forecast a future occurrence, consistent with the hypothesis.

EXPERIMENT: Carry out a test to see if predicted event occurs.

- If results DO match prediction, hypothesis is supported (but not proved).

- If results DO NOT match prediction,

RECYCLE

REVISED HYPOTHESIS → **PREDICTION** → **EXPERIMENT**

If results do match prediction, hypothesis is supported.

If results DO NOT match prediction → **RECYCLE**

FIGURE 7-4. The Method of Science Revisited

CHAPTER EIGHT

Benefit/Risk Analysis

Potential Applications of Scientific Knowledge

No theory is good except on condition that
one uses it to go beyond.

André Gide

Life forms have profoundly transformed the environment
in which they live. For example, Earth's present-day atmosphere was created by the actions of oxygen-producing
plants and nitrogen-producing bacteria. These actions were
not the result of conscious decisions; they were simply
physiological responses.

Only one life form is capable of making complex conscious decisions: humans. As human societies evolved, so
did ethics and values, dimensions that helped shape human
behavior. To understand the potential impact of scientific
ideas, it is necessary to examine how these dimensions
arose and what role they play in making decisions about applications of scientific knowledge.

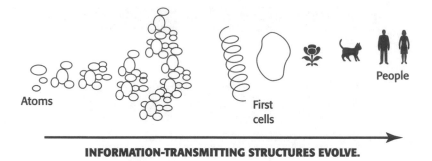

INFORMATION-TRANSMITTING STRUCTURES EVOLVE.

FIGURE 8-1. Evolution of Structures for Transmitting Information

Hey, I'm Me!

The chief indicator of the evolutionary process that took place on Earth was the evolution of structures for transmitting information, most notably the DNA molecule. And eventually, people evolved, as illustrated in Figure 8-1.

Somewhere along this path of evolution, what might be called *simple people* (people-as-organisms, people-as-animals) became aware of their own existence—they realized that they were. Jesuit philosopher Teilhard de Chardin has called humankind "evolution become conscious of itself." People-become-conscious-of-themselves added a new dimension to evolution, personal self-consciousness; and simple people became more complex people (people-as-rational/emotional-beings) as illustrated in Figure 8-2.

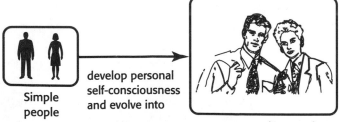

FIGURE 8-2. Evolution of Personal Self-Consciousness

Information that went beyond that conveyed by DNA structures came into play. Human beings not only knew, they *knew* that they knew. Complex people, though still partly directed by their DNA, also became directed by their consciousness—their image of themselves. Evolution continued as the structures for transmitting information (DNA) were coupled with heightened development of personal self-consciousness. (*Evolution* in this sense is the cumulative increase of knowledge.)

Hey, We're Us!

As evolution continued, people formed simple societies. These simple societies eventually evolved into more complex societies. As these societies occupied the various parts of the Earth, they formed increasingly complex societies that became aware of themselves and others. Power and power structures developed along with systems for the exchange of goods.

As shown in Figure 8-3, a new dimension of knowledge accompanied the development of social groups or societies: social self-consciousness—society's awareness of its own existence. As awareness and complexity increased, members of one society began to step out of their own social skins, so to speak, and to look at themselves and their own society from the outside. You might have experienced social self-consciousness if you have traveled abroad and were confronted by your national identity when someone said you were "acting like an American (or Belgian, or Japanese, or . . .)."

Who Wrote the Rules?

Ethics arose as a result of the appearance of human personal and social self-consciousness, when humans found they had to make conscious choices of action in a social context. Modern ethical codes evolved from survival-oriented rules that applied to the individual. The rules were extended to deal with the family and then the tribe. In many cases, elaborate

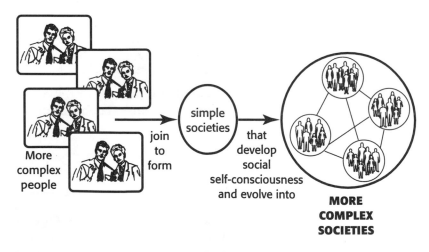

FIGURE 8-3. Evolution of Social Self-Consciousness

rules governed relationships between members of the same tribe; however, if a member of another tribe was encountered, the rules did not apply. The outsider could be enslaved or killed. The extension of ethical principles to larger groupings continued as civilizations developed.

It would be nice to have an "ethical method" comparable to the scientific method. Because moral rules act as plans enabling one human being to know what to expect from another, it would be fortunate if there was a means by which personal and societal moral conflicts could be resolved. There is, however, no such thing as an "all-encompassing ethical method." The basic difficulty inhibiting the development of an ethical method is that ethical rules are the free choice of every individual; individuals are free to modify or change their ethical standards on the basis of their own experiences. There is no comparable choice in the sciences, for science's method is a self-correcting mechanism in which predictions accurately carry the truth or falsity of the hypothesis to an ultimate test, an experiment based on the hypothesis.

Though beliefs about values are not amenable to strict experimental testing, they nevertheless make predictions of a sort, namely, that if a certain ethical theory or rule is put into practice, a future valued world will come about. The test here is whether the application does make a better world. If it does, the successful application helps the belief to persist. Wisdom achieved through experiences of this sort can be used to develop newer (recycled) ethical theories.

Despite the differences between them, scientific and ethical beliefs are frequently interwoven, for ethical beliefs are *required* in the making of moral (value-laden) decisions about the application of scientific (value-free) knowledge. Decisions about questions such as whether knowledge about the structure of atoms *ought* to be utilized to design, fabricate, and deploy nuclear weapons necessarily involve ethical value judgments. In the discussions that precede such decisions, discussions that often involve conflicting ethical beliefs, *it is essential to identify the various ethical beliefs and to separate them from the scientific ones.*

Benefits and Risks: Inseparable Pair

Scientific understandings and human values are links in the chain of reasoning that must be used when making decisions about potential technological applications, as illustrated in Figure 8-4.

Decisions about whether to commit resources to a project involve a reasoning process used often in day-to-day living. When considering whether to proceed with a proposed action, a person tries to figure out what potential benefits might result from the action and what potential risks are involved. This technique, which is known as *benefit/risk analysis,* considers what can be gained and what can be lost if such an action is taken.

- If, *according to one's value system,* it can be determined that a lot more can be gained than lost, then the decision is usually made to commit resources (time, money, land, etc.) to the proposed action.
- If, *according to one's value system,* it can be determined that a lot more can be lost than gained, then the decision is usually made not to proceed.
- If, *according to one's value system,* the loss is about equal to the gain, then the decision is usually made not to proceed. Most of the time, the expectation of considerably more gains than losses are required in order for the risks associated with a proposed action to be accepted. When state lottery prizes reach multimillion dollar figures, people who would not risk a

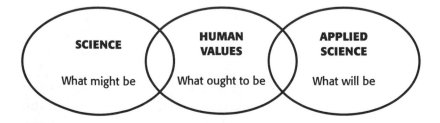

FIGURE 8-4. Links in a Chain of Reasoning

© The New Yorker Magazine, Inc.

single dollar in the hope of doubling their money gamble *thousands* of dollars.

The Three Biggest Resources: Energy, Matter, and Information

Scientific ideas are just ideas until it is time to decide whether to apply them. Decisions about applied science are essentially decisions about the use of the three major planetary resources: energy, matter, and information. With regard to *energy,* the Earth is an *open system* because it continually imports energy from the sun in the form of electromagnetic radiation and converts it into other types of energy. For example, the energy from the sun continues to make it possible for ocean water to evaporate and form clouds, which eventually deposit rain in mountains, from whence the water flows downstream where it can be harnessed to produce hydroelectric energy before reentering the ocean.

With regard to *matter,* the Earth is virtually a *closed system.* Aside from occasional meteorites entering our atmosphere and the minor loss of atoms from the upper atmosphere, the amount of matter on Earth is fixed. This makes the Earth like a spaceship traveling around the sun. Matter gets shifted around, reformulated, utilized, and, not infrequently, abandoned. When matter is accessible and useful, it is a *resource;* when it is in the wrong place at the wrong time in the wrong concentration, it is a *pollutant.*

Information, the third major planetary resource, has the potential of being almost limitless. Human intelligence augmented by machines such as computers holds forth the promise of neverending expansion of the knowledge base. As long as there are humans, there will be knowledge potential.

Using Benefit/Risk Analysis

The following sections illustrate examples involving potential uses of each of the three resources and how benefit/risk analysis can be used to help make decisions about applications of scientific knowledge.

A good way to start is to state a broad initial proposition that is as extreme as possible, to examine the benefits and risks of the proposed action, and then to compare this proposition with less extreme ones. Think of the proposition as a general policy statement or platform, the details of which will be worked out later by a committee.

The first example presents some of the unavoidable decisions that must be made in setting energy priorities. The second example shows how a scientific panacea like chlorofluorocarbon spray-can propellants can turn into a scientific nightmare. The third example shows how computerized credit and banking information, an application of scientific knowledge, can permeate everyday life, sometimes for good and sometimes for bad.

Each of these examples involves critical decisions about the evolving environment within which life forms dwell and without which life forms cease to exist. They deal with decisions that might determine whether future generations inherit planet that is habitable. They deal with a frustrating paradox: Efforts to improve living standards are themselves beginning to threaten global health.

Benefits and Risks of Utilizing Energy Resources

Today's society require large amounts of *energy*, which is defined as the capacity to do work. Energy is the ultimate currency of modern civilization. Without a plentiful supply, transportation, agriculture, industry, urban development, and numerous other human activities would have to be seriously curtailed. As a result, there is a constant process of locating additional supplies of energy resources now in use and, at the same time, developing new sources of energy.

The five biggest ideas of science can be useful in developing needed energy resources.

- Physics' model of the atom has led to the alteration of atomic structures to produce nuclear energy on a large scale.
- Chemistry's periodic law has aided in the selection of elements for use in improved fuels.
- Astronomy's Big Bang theory has led to attempts to reproduce fusion reactions, which heat the sun, to provide energy for earthly uses.
- Geology's plate tectonics model has pinpointed subsurface heat energy that can be harnessed as geothermal energy.
- Biology's theory of evolution has provided information about sources of energy-rich fossils for use as fuels.

Accompanying the difficulties in developing sufficient energy resources, the recurrent "energy crisis," is an environmental crisis. Air is unfit to breathe in some places, water is not safe to drink in others, and poisons contaminate fish and cattle elsewhere. Much of the pollution can be traced to the burning of fuels, so there is a direct link between pollution and the energy problem. Furthermore, efforts to clean up pollution expend additional energy and, thus, create additional pollution. This energy-pollution *cycle* is a vicious circle (see Figure 8-5).

Societies clearly have to act *now* to make energy production and use more efficient and to limit extravagant consumption. Benefit/risk analysis can be used to help guide these actions.

"THEY REVISED IT. NOW IT'S THE 'PRETTY-CLEAN AIR ACT'."

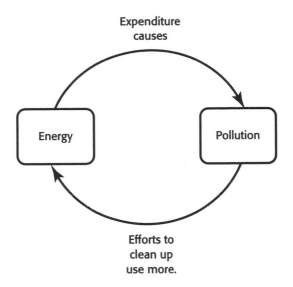

Figure 8-5. Energy-Pollution Cycle

INITIAL PROPOSITION   Energy conservation should be mandatory, with strict limits on usage and stiff penalties for violators.

Benefits

- Curtailed burning of fossil fuels such as coal and petroleum would reduce potentially harmful effects on the global climate.
- Curtailed destruction of forests would help prevent extinction of species dependent on forest environments.
- The less energy used, the less pollution created, and the healthier people will be.
- Mandatory conservation would work. Voluntary conservation has not worked well.
- Products derived from petroleum (lubricants, plastics, medicines) will be available longer if conservation is practiced.

Risks

- Costly and inconvenient conservation measures are not really necessary because there is no real shortage.
- Mandatory controls infringe on freedom of the individual.
- *Not* having to set up the control mechanisms required for a mandatory system avoids creation of a larger and more inefficient bureaucracy.
- The alternatives to the present highly consumptive lifestyles are insufficiently developed, and mandatory conservation measures would cause serious hardships and economic dislocations for all. (For example, many cities lack good local mass transportation.)
- Enforcement and allocation systems would be susceptible to corruption.

MODIFIED PROPOSITION   Energy conservation should be *voluntary*, with generous financial *incentives* for those who cooperate. Voluntary actions might prove more effective than mandated ones, especially if incentives for compliance are offered. The end result of such deliberations and refinements can be an energy policy that has worldwide implications, for better or for worse.

Benefits and Risks of Using Chlorofluorocarbon Spray-Can Propellants

Scientific knowledge has made possible such modern-day miracles as wonder drugs, earth-orbiting satellites, and pest-resistant crops. Unfortunately, some of the supposed miracles have turned out to be mixed blessings. Sometimes, there are advance warnings of the dangers. Other times, the problems are totally unanticipated.

An example of the latter situation involves the design of propellants for aerosol spray cans, which serve to transport chemicals such as hair spray, deodorants, and disinfectants.

Spray cans require a *propellant*—a gas that propels the chemicals to their destinations (hair, etc.) Ideally, the propellant should be odorless, nonflammable, noncorrosive, and nontoxic.

In the 1930s, chemists developed *chlorofluorocarbon propellants* (CFCs)—molecules containing atoms of chlorine, fluorine, and carbon. CFCs had all of the ideal properties for a propellant and, therefore, were considered a chemist's dream. Several decades later, the dream became a nightmare because of unanticipated effects of CFCs in the atmosphere. These effects involve the function of one component of the atmosphere, ozone, O_3, which is formed high in the atmosphere. Ozone is found in significant concentrations in an ozone layer, or ozonosphere, that is observed at heights from 6 to 30 miles above the Earth's surface (see Figure 8-6). Ozone is continually formed and destroyed by various processes occurring in this layer.

The ozonosphere is of particular significance to life on Earth because it serves to shield the Earth's surface from ultraviolet (UV) radiation. There is strong evidence that UV radiation can induce skin cancers; thus, an increase in UV radiation would result in an increase in the number of skin

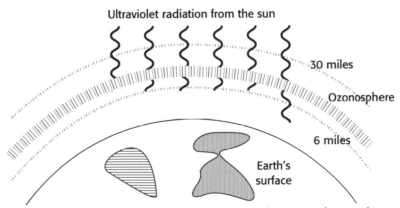

Most of the ultraviolet radiation is blocked by the ozonosphere and never reaches the Earth's surface.

FIGURE 8-6. The Ozonosphere

cancers. Increased UV radiation has also been shown to increase the human birth-defect rate. It might also cause mutations in plant life that could significantly decrease the population of oxygen-producing plants in the sea. In this scenario, less oxygen would be produced, which eventually might lead to the extinction of all oxygen-breathing life.

Chemical reactions involving ozone have been studied intensively in research laboratories. It has been observed that chlorofluorocarbon molecules can cause the destruction of ozone molecules. In 1974, Professors Rowland and Molina, two chemists at the University of California, analyzed the implications of these observations and proposed the Rowland-Molina chlorofluorocarbon-ozone depletion model. This hypothesis states that chlorofluorocarbon gases are in the process of reducing the ozone present in the ozonosphere, resulting in a serious health hazard for people. Rowland and Molina reasoned that although CFCs are inert under conditions at the surface of the Earth, when they rise up to the ozone layer, the intense radiation there causes the CFCs to break apart. The fragments produced then facilitate destruction of ozone molecules.

The seriousness of the situation was difficult to estimate. The exact relationship between excessive radiation and living things was not clear. Furthermore, it was alleged by the producers of these aerosols that the rate of ozone depletion is far slower than the rate assumed by the two chemists in their calculations. Thus, some argued, the effect, if any, might not be significant. The producers contended that the chemistry of the upper atmosphere is so complex that the significance of the chlorofluorocarbon-ozone reactions could not be estimated accurately. They said that many other processes occurring in this layer might offset whatever depletion of ozone is caused by chlorofluorocarbons. They urged continued sampling of the upper atmosphere to test the hypothesis' predictions. They argued that, even if the effect was measurable, a number of years would be needed to assess the extent of the danger.

Rowland and Molina's hypothesis stimulated intense debate about CFC use. Benefit/risk analysis can be used to examine the arguments involved. (Again, the initial proposition should be as extreme as possible.)

INITIAL PROPOSITION   Chlorofluorocarbon propellant spray cans should be banned totally and immediately.

Benefits

- Eliminate possibility of CFCs causing increase of human skin cancer rate.
- Eliminate danger of CFCs causing increase in human birth-defect rate.
- Decrease possibility of CFCs causing extinction of all oxygen-breathing life.

Risks

- Loss of push-button convenience.
- Loss of profit for companies involved.
- Loss of fine-spray control in medical applications.
- Loss of jobs for some workers in this industry.

"TRUE, THE CHLOROFLUOROCARBON INDUSTRY'S THREAT TO THE OZONE LAYER MAY VERY WELL BE SERIOUS, BUT THE OZONE LAYER'S THREAT TO THE CHLOROFLUOROCARBON INDUSTRY IS EQUALLY SERIOUS."

"OH, FOR PETE'S SAKE, LET'S JUST GET SOME OZONE AND SEND IT BACK UP THERE!"

MODIFIED PROPOSITION Chlorofluorocarbon propellant spray cans should be partially banned, exempting medical uses; a worker retraining and relocation program should be started to lessen economic impact. A partial and gradual ban might be more feasible, especially as time is needed to develop propellant substitutes and alternate jobs. Deliberations about this issue have produced CFC usage policies that can rid our planet of this potentially *lethal* threat.

Benefits and Risks of Utilizing Computerized Credit and Banking Information

Modern societies require large amounts of information. For this reason, computers have become indispensable in the operation of these societies. Computers have evolved in the same way that life forms evolved: from the simple to the complex. Evolution of a new computer generation becomes possible because of technological developments that result in greatly increased speed of operation and decreased size.

The enormous storage capacity, speed of calculations, automatic nature, and decreasing cost of operation of computers have combined to make them an integral part of today's environment. Computers now make possible the storage of vast amounts of personal, governmental, and business information. Because of the large-scale potential for use and abuse of this information, decisions must be made about who should have access to it and what restrictions, if any, should be placed on how that information can be used.

One such application is electronic fund transfer (EFT). In an EFT system, a bank issues a person a debit card that he or she turns over to a clerk when making a purchase. The clerk can use the card in a terminal to automatically charge the bank account of the customer and credit the store's bank account. This creates a record not only of the amount but also of the item purchased.

When EFT is fully functional throughout the country (or world), there will be a centralized computerized databank for just about all families. Access to any of the terminals leading to this databank can provide access to information about the purchasing patterns of these families. This information could be used, for example, to target certain families for direct advertising. Of course, safeguards can be put in place; but, as is often the case, computer hackers can find ways to circumvent the safeguards.

Detailed and sensitive information is available *right now* to financial institutions and merchants who wish to evaluate potential customers. Master files already exist that contain information such as people's real estate holdings, the value of their homes, their children's ages, and even their neighbors' phone numbers!

The present level of computer development is such that a centralized databank could be maintained with information about each individual in the United States, listing current bank balances and including recent credits and

"WE HAVE SOME FACTS ABOUT YOU THAT YOU DON'T REMEMBER, SOME THAT YOU THOUGHT WERE REALLY SECRET, AND SOME THAT NEVER EVEN HAPPENED."

debits in any bank, savings and loan, credit card company, store, and so on. Would such a databank be desirable? (Again, begin with an extreme initial proposition.)

INITIAL PROPOSITION　A centralized computerized banking and credit databank should be maintained to include information about every individual, with unlimited access granted to financial institutions and merchants.

Benefits

- This would cut down on processing of bad checks, currently a significant business cost.
- Total accounting costs would decrease because there would be less duplication of effort.
- More convenient checking procedures for merchants would cut down unauthorized credit card use.
- Ready availability of balances would help eliminate some of the difficulties in personal record keeping.

Risks

- Access to these files would compromise the individual's right to privacy.
- Unauthorized access could lead to harassment of individuals.
- Errors could lead to serious misunderstandings and embarrassment of individuals.
- Centralization makes widespread fraud more possible because of increased access to so many individual accounts.

MODIFIED PROPOSITION Instead of giving a customer's bank balance, the computer would simply authorize or not authorize a purchase based upon the customer having sufficient funds. This would serve to partially protect an individual's privacy.

A nationwide or even worldwide databank containing a massive pool of information might soon become a reality. When and if such a databank is implemented, privacy rights and other considerations must be weighed against the legitimate information needs of industry. The longer decisions about this issue are delayed, the more widespread and entrenched the abuse of such information will become.

Scientific Ideas and Our Image of the Future

People all over the world look up at the stars. Beneath those stars, they see cloud formations. And beneath those cloud formations, they see where sky and Earth meet. There, they see life forms that have taken hold on this planet—plants that live in the ocean and plants that have developed into forests; animals that ingest plants and animals that eat other animals.

It took billions of years for the plant and animal life on Earth to develop. It took just several thousand years for human beings to develop civilizations that now share the

Earth with those plants and animals. Civilizations have the power to use scientific ideas to alter the clouds and the sky and the Earth and the plants and the animals in ways that are unprecedented in the history of this planet. Human beings have the power to improve *or* worsen the fragile ecosystems that support life on this Earth and to improve quality of life *or* to worsen it.

Humans are uniquely endowed with the ability to use this power to create a future that they can *imagine*—dreams *can* come true. Therefore, images of the future must be evaluated with great care to guard against the "unpredicted" backfiring on everyone. The power of scientific ideas must be used as wisely as possible, for any decisions will affect not only this generation, but also generations to come.

Idea Folders

36 Global Warning: Radiative Equilibrium

37 Geothermal Energy

38 Disposal of Unwanted By-Products

39 Genesis of the Ozone Layer: Chemical Equilibrium

40 Smaller and Faster Computers: Biochips, Atomchips, and Spinchips

Epilogue

If a botanist took you on a field trip to a forest, he or she would invite you to see the variety of forest plants. The botanist might point out, for example, the relationship between the amount of sunlight that reaches portions of the forest floor and the types of plants found there.

If a painter took you on a field trip to a forest, she or he would invite you to see the variety of forest colors. The

painter might point out, for example, the relationship between the amount of sunlight that reaches portions of the
forest floor and the richness of the colors found there.

These varieties of plants and colors were there all the
time, but you might not have noticed them without the help
of the botanist and the painter. These people opened your
eyes to new perceptions. They taught you how to see the
forest in new ways.

As each new pattern was revealed, you achieved a new
gestalt of the forest. "Gestalt" refers to the act of perception
in which an entire pattern suddenly becomes evident. Plate
tectonics was a gestalt switch from a static Earth model; the
heliocentric model was a gestalt switch from the geocentric
model. Once these gestalts are yours, the world will never
look the same.

Along with scientific and esthetic gestalts of the world, there are ethical dimensions and ethical gestalts, gestalts that have been called means of ensuring that what is attractive in the short term is weighed in the balance of the ultimate, long-term satisfaction. Scientific, esthetic, and ethical gestalts each contribute to a comprehensive gestalt of the universe.

A gestalt is sometimes referred to as the "Aha!" phenomenon, like the "Aha!" that Sherlock Holmes says when he has figured out who the criminal is or that you utter when you finally figure out what the whispering for the last few days and the cars parked down the street have been all about: a surprise birthday party! Sometimes the "Aha!" experience can result from the "ha ha" experience, as when Sidney's humor provides a new point of view and you get the joke.

The five biggest ideas were chosen because of their all-encompassing explanatory power, their all-encompassing gestalt. We hope our prose and Sidney's cartoons have given you some worthwhile "Aha!" and "ha ha" experiences.

Idea Folders

Introduction

Idea folders are brief discussions of interesting topics related to the five biggest ideas, as well as introductions to other scientific ideas. They are arranged in the same order as the chapters, and each folder is referenced at least once in a chapter.

We hope they satisfy your curiosity, or pique it. You can "open" a folder, or learn more about the topic, by consulting the Additional Reading selections or other books about science.

◰ 1 ◱ Philosophical Presuppositions of Science

Before scientific thinking can proceed, certain philosophical presuppositions must be made about the nature of the universe:

- ◑ Objective reality exists—there really are things out there, everything is not simply a figment of the imagination.
- ◑ The universe is knowable—no aspects of the universe are beyond human understanding.
- ◑ The universe's operation is regular and predictable— if events occur at random, without any warning or pattern, no amount of analysis will uncover any regularity to them.

Although the validity of these presuppositions is not completely established, the official attitude of science is to suspend judgment on such matters and to go ahead and construct scientific ideas. This procedure, often called *operationalism,* allows science to progress, even though questions about its logical underpinnings are not yet settled.

2 Serendipity and Progress in Science

When using the scientific method, scientists do not always find what they expect to find; their predictions are not always borne out. Their payoff in this situation is the discovery that the hypothesis on which the prediction was based needs to be modified.

Sometimes, accidental discoveries of things not sought result in an even greater payoff: The discovery itself is valuable. This phenomenon is known as *serendipity*.

Such discoveries are not mere accidents. One needs the appropriate background to recognize a discovery as valuable. Louis Pasteur, who made many important scientific breakthroughs, acknowledged this when he said, "In the fields of observation, chance favors only the prepared mind."

A classic example of serendipity is the discovery of the vulcanization process for rubber. In 1839, Charles Goodyear accidentally dropped a piece of rubber mixed with sulfur onto a hot stove and discovered that the rubber took on some of the sought-after properties of leather—strength, elasticity, and resistance to solvents. Vulcanization also rendered the rubber impervious to moderate heat and cold. The invention of vulcanization made possible the wide use of rubber and aided the development of such industries as the automobile industry.

3 | Occam's Razor at Work: Space Travelers from the Past

Reports about events that supposedly took place in the distant past have led some to suggest hypotheses about the long ago visitation of Earth by space travelers from other planets. Science cannot adequately evaluate such theories until conditions for the application of the scientific method can be fulfilled—there must be some possibility of experimentation that could either support or falsify these ideas.

In the absence of such experimental evidence, the simplest hypothesis, one that explains past events without including actions of space travelers, is tentatively accepted as the most likely. Regardless of the past accomplishments of the proposer of an untestable hypothesis, or the number of people who agree with it, or the popularity of books supporting it, science will not officially dignify it as a scientific theory.

4 | BIG and SMALL Things

The range of sizes of objects, masses, and time in the universe is so wide that special means are used in expressing them to avoid confusion and to facilitate discussion. Prefixes are used in the metric system to stand for multiples or fractions of base units, all of which are powers (multiples) of ten. Here's a listing of some of them, with examples of how they are used:

- *nano* = one billionth = 10^{-9} (computer processing times—*nanoseconds*)
- *micro* = one millionth = 10^{-6} (smallest sizes seen by a microscope—*micrometers*)
- *milli* = one thousandth = 10^{-3} (fat content of foods—*milligrams*)
- *centi* = one hundredth = 10^{-2} (temperature scale—*centigrade*)
- *kilo* = one thousand = 10^{+3} (standard unit of mass—*kilogram*)
- *mega* = one million = 10^{+6} (computer memory—*megabytes*)
- *giga* = one billion = 10^{+9} (computer hard drives—*gigabytes*)

5 | Electromagnetic Radiation and Its Interaction with Matter

When electric charges are accelerated, they produce a disturbance in the electromagnetic field, which then propagates as a wave in the electromagnetic field, for example, visible light. All light waves travel at the same speed in a vacuum (3×10^8 meters per second) but differ from each other in frequency and wavelength. Radio waves, microwaves, and infrared (IR) radiation all have lower frequencies (and longer wavelengths) than visible light. Ultraviolet (UV) radiation, X rays, and gamma rays have higher frequencies (and shorter wavelengths) than visible light.

The interaction between light and matter depends on the frequency match between the light wave and the natural frequency of the molecules in the matter. If the frequencies are widely different, the molecules do not respond to the light, and light is either transmitted or absorbed by the matter in the form of heat energy. If the frequencies are close, the molecules resonate, absorbing and reradiating the electromagnetic energy. For example, in matter that appears to be red in color, the molecules that make up the matter have natural frequencies in the red region of the visible spectrum. When white light (light containing all visible wavelength frequencies) falls on this material, the molecules selectively absorb and reradiate red light waves.

6 Wave Model versus Particle Model of Light

Light has been viewed in two fundamentally different forms: waves and particles. The wave model was favored initially because it was needed to explain such phenomena as diffraction (an initially straight light wave front moving through a small opening in a barrier becomes spherical) and interference (more than one light wave occupy the same space at the same time).

The advent of quantum theory allowed light to be viewed as a particle because light interacted with electrons in such a way that particle collision theory accurately described the events.

To add to the confusion, the physicist Louis deBroglie suggested that things normally thought of as particles could behave, under some conditions, like waves. Experimental confirmation followed shortly: Electrons, neutrons, and even whole sodium atoms underwent diffraction and interference.

The modern view is that light, and matter as well, cannot be described by simple wave or particle models. In fact, they are something else, more sophisticated than either, and not fully capable of description by current concepts.

7   An Enlarged Atom: Flies Buzzing around Billiard Balls

How might an atom look if it could actually be seen? If an atom could somehow be enlarged to the point where the protons in the nucleus were the size and mass of billiard balls, then the size and mass of the electrons would be about the same as fruit flies. If the closely packed billiard-ball nucleus was placed at the 50-yard line of a modern football stadium, the fly-electrons would be orbiting at a distance corresponding to the outer edge of the stadium parking lots.

Because electrons can absorb only particular (quantized) amounts of energy from their surroundings, in the scaled-up atom, the flies would quite suddenly start orbiting the billiard balls at further distances. When the fly-electron made the transition back to a smaller orbit, it would resemble a tiny firefly because it would give off energy in the form of light.

8 Schrödinger's Cat: A Thought Experiment

Quantum mechanics created some interesting philosophical questions about reality. According to the older, Newtonian picture, there is just one universe, and the behavior of anything at some later time can be predicted with certainty as long as the conditions at an earlier time and the forces acting on the object are known.

Quantum mechanics changed the Newtonian picture in revolutionary ways. To illustrate, consider the thought experiment known as "Schrödinger's Cat." A cat is put into a sealed chamber with a mechanism for releasing poison gas. The gas is either released or not released as a result of the occurrence or nonoccurrence of some random event in the physical world, such as the spontaneous decay of a radioactive nucleus. What is the status of the cat at the end of the experiment?

According to the classical, Newtonian thought, the cat is either alive or dead—actually knowing whether the cat is alive or dead has no bearing on the outcome. According to the Copenhagen Interpretation of Quantum Mechanics, because there is some probability of the cat being alive and some probability of it being dead, the cat exists in a kind of limbo state and only becomes really alive or really dead when the box is opened and its real state revealed. In the Many Worlds Interpretation, the instant the box is opened, the universe splits into two separate states: In one of these, there is the observer and a live cat, and, in the other, the observer and a dead cat!

9 Heisenberg's Uncertainty Principle

Another idea that flows from quantum mechanics is that the very act of observation alters the phenomenon being observed. For example, think about how the moon is observed in its orbit around the Earth. The sun gives off light, which bounces off the moon. The observer receives that light and then traces its path back to the moon to determine the moon's location. The wavelength of the light is much smaller than the size of the moon, a fact that allows the moon's position to be determined accurately. The infinitesimal amount of pressure exerted by the sunlight on the moon does not affect the moon's orbit materially.

On the other hand, attempting to determine the orbit of an electron involves bouncing off the electron electromagnetic radiation having a smaller wavelength than visible light. (Visible light cannot be used because it has too long a wavelength in relation to the size of an electron to yield any useful information about the electron's position.) The smaller the wavelength, the larger the energy of the radiation. Thus, the greater the accuracy demanded for locating the electron's position, the greater the energy of the radiation used to detect it, and the greater the disturbance of the electron's orbit. In the limiting case, the electron's position was known precisely, but it has been disturbed so much that it is no longer there!

10 Matter versus Antimatter

Every particle is believed to have an *antiparticle*—a particle having the same mass as the first particle but opposite in other features. In 1928, the electron was postulated to have such an antiparticle. This antiparticle was found in 1932 and called the *positron* because it had a positive charge. Soon other antiparticles were found, leading to the idea that there could be antiatoms, antisolids, antiplanets, antistars, and so on. Because the existence of antimatter at a distance cannot easily be detected, it is not clear how much antimatter exists in the universe.

The interaction of ordinary matter and antimatter is a violent one, resulting in an annihilation in which the masses are converted into energy in the form of gamma rays. Whether a planet is made of matter or antimatter will be a critical factor in the decision of an astronaut to land or not land on an unexplored planet!

11　Scanning Tunneling Microscopy: "Seeing" Atoms

Recent breakthroughs in the field of microscopy have provided evidence for the apparent reality of atoms. In the
1950s, images of gas atoms striking a fluorescent screen were
produced. In 1976, the *thermal motion* of uranium atoms was
seen. Then, in 1981, with the development of a new family of
microscopes called scanned-probe microscopes (such as the
scanning tunneling microscope), sensing of *entities* with *properties consistent with atoms* was achieved.

Scanned-probe technique is based on the observation that the
current that flows between a probe, such as the tip of a sharp
piece of tungsten metal, and the surface over which it is moved
is very sensitive to the distance between the tip and the metal
surface. It is so sensitive that variations on the order of atomic
sizes can be distinguished. A metal tip is scanned over a surface and raised up or down as needed to keep the current constant. The constancy of the current implies a constant distance
between the probe and the surface, so displacements of the
metal tip yield a topographic picture of the surface.

12 The Four Basic Forces in Nature

As currently viewed by physics, there are four fundamental forces in nature:

- ◑ Strong nuclear—the strongest force; works at short ranges of 10^{-15} meters or less.
- ◑ Weak nuclear—only 10^{-8} of the strong-nuclear force strength; works at ranges of 10^{-17} meters or less.
- ◑ Electromagnetic—10^{-3} of the strong-nuclear force strength; works at all ranges.
- ◑ Gravitational—weakest, at 10^{-45} of the strong-nuclear force strength; works at all ranges.

Actually, the electromagnetic and the weak nuclear forces have been combined into a single force—the electroweak force. A further combination of the strong nuclear force and the electroweak force into a single force is proposed in the Grand Unified Theory (GUT), which also includes the possibility of a further combination with the gravitational force into a single superforce.

13 Electricity and Magnetism: Siamese Twins

Few connections were made between electricity and magnetism until the nineteenth century. Today, it is known that they have much in common. A stationary electric charge is surrounded by an electric field. When in motion, it is also surrounded by a magnetic field. Similarly, a fixed magnet is surrounded by a magnetic field. Whenever the magnetic field varies, it induces an electric field, in a phenomenon called *electromagnetic induction.*

Magnetism is a property of matter that is determined by how the atoms in a particular solid are arranged relative to one another and how the electron magnetic fields of the various atoms are aligned. A permanent magnet is an object that has its atoms and electron fields frozen into a particular pattern. Although the Earth behaves as though it were a simple permanent bar magnet oriented north and south through the center of the Earth, its magnetic field is most likely that of an electromagnet.

14 Newton's Laws of Motion and Gravitation

Isaac Newton's laws of motion are truly big ideas because they describe all motion in the everyday world. With these laws, he could describe both kinds of motion recognized by scientists: uniform (nonaccelerated) and accelerated.

Newton also worked out the idea of *universal gravitation:* Every body in the universe attracts every other body, and the force of attraction is related to the masses of the objects involved and the distance between them. It is this gravitational force that keeps planets in their orbits, holds the material around the cores of stars, and binds stars together in galaxies.

A modern application of Newton's laws of motion and gravitation is provided by the design of *geosynchronous satellites—* satellites that remain in the same location above the Earth. If a satellite is launched from Earth in precisely the correct direction and with just the right speed, its orbital period will match the Earth's rotation rate. This produces a satellite that is held in place by the gravitational force at a particular point above the Earth. Signals can be beamed at the satellite, then rebroadcast to a wider area, yet still stay within the line-of-sight transmission boundaries.

15 Einstein's Theories of Special and General Relativity

Developed by Einstein just after the turn of the twentieth century, the theory of special relativity regards the speed of light to be a more fundamental constant than space and time themselves. Einstein said that, regardless of the motion of the source or the motion of the observer, the speed of light in free space will have the same value to all observers. This theory agrees with an experimental result of Michelson and Morley, which could not be explained any other way.

The theory was truly revolutionary and a truly big idea in science. But because of the extremely high speeds involved in its application, it is outside the normal experience of human beings. It is counterintuitive, which led early students of relativity to remark about its incomprehensibility. In fact, the theory is not that hard to understand at a mathematical level.

Special relativity is called *special* because it deals with uniform (nonaccelerated) motion only. Einstein's theory of general relativity is called *general* because it includes accelerated as well as nonaccelerated motion. General relativity theory includes the idea that gravity causes space to become curved and time to slow down.

16 Radioisotopes as Tracers

Radioactive isotopes or radioisotopes can be used by scientists to trace the path of the atoms of an element in a physical, chemical, or biological process. When used for this purpose, the radioisotopes are called tracers.

An example of using radioisotopes as tracers in a physical process is the locating of the site of a leak in a pipe buried beneath a concrete floor. Instead of digging up extensive areas of the floor to find the leak, a radioisotope can be added to the liquid going into the pipe. A Geiger counter (an instrument that detects and measures radioactivity) can be used to locate the place where the liquid is escaping.

17 Organic versus Inorganic Chemistry

There are presently about 112 known elements. It might seem surprising that one branch of chemistry, organic chemistry, is devoted to the study of the compounds of just a single element—carbon—whereas inorganic chemistry studies all the other elements. The reason for this is that carbon can form more compounds than any other element. It has a unique ability to form covalent bonds (bonds in which pairs of electrons are shared) with other carbon atoms in a seemingly endless array of combinations.

The name *organic* is a relic of the past. About 150 years ago, scientists believed that life-sustaining carbon compounds could be made only within living organisms. They were consequently called organic compounds. It is now known that organic compounds can be synthesized in the laboratory from simple inorganic (nonorganic) substances. Today, over 8 million synthetic and natural organic compounds are known.

18 A Relatively Short Observation Time

Scientists have been making detailed telescopic observations of the universe for about 400 years. How can the small fraction of the total lifetime of the universe be put into perspective? It would correspond to a 3- or 4-second examination of an adult, from which the doctor then made detailed pronouncements about the adult's birth process, infancy, early childhood, teenage years, and even time and cause of eventual death!

From another perspective, suppose the total lifetime of the universe were a single 24-hour day. Then, starting at midnight, Earth would have appeared at 4 P.M., the first fossils would have formed at 10 P.M., humans would have appeared at 11:59:58 P.M. (2 seconds before midnight), and the first telescopic observations would have been made at 0.003 seconds before midnight.

19 Visible versus Nonvisible Astronomies

Ordinary telescopes can enhance the ability of the unaided eye to see celestial objects. Unfortunately, the atmosphere gets in the way, scattering the light from distant stars, causing "twinkling" and even totally obscuring the view when clouds cover the sky.

To help solve problems caused by the atmosphere, instruments have been devised to detect regions of the spectrum other than the visible. The first such region to be explored was the radiowave region. In the 1930s, Karl Jansky set up receivers to scan the sky in the radio-frequency band. Although this produced new information, the long wavelength in this band did not permit much resolution.

Other wavelengths did not penetrate the atmosphere, so sensors were sent aloft with balloons and rockets to get above much of the atmosphere for clearer viewing. Eventually, satellites were used to get instruments above most of the atmosphere, and the sky was mapped in the ultraviolet (UV), X ray, and infrared (IR) regions of the spectrum. Most recently, the Hubble space telescope was put into an orbit from which it is able to detect visible as well as other regions of the spectrum.

20 Estimating the Age of the Universe

A major goal of astronomy has been to determine the age of the universe. Astronomers have been forced to accept imprecise estimates because of uncertainties in the data used in their calculations.

One technique for making estimates involves running the expansion of the universe in reverse, as though it were a movie film. In the reversed movie, instead of moving away from each other, galaxies approach one another. The age of the universe in this scenario is the time it takes for the galaxies to meet simultaneously, re-creating the primeval fireball. Assuming that the rate at which the universe is now expanding has been constant (and, thus, the rate in reversal is constant), the age of the universe can be calculated from the distances separating the galaxies now and the rate at which the universe is expanding. According to early data, the age of the universe was estimated at 2 billion years. But this value was inconsistent with the Earth's estimated age of over 4 billion years! Subsequent data gave the universe an age of about 20 billion years.

Recently, the previously accepted age of the universe came under serious question because of more precise data obtained from the Hubble space telescope. These data resulted in a much lower estimated age, 12 to 15 billion years. This age has created a crisis in astronomy as earlier estimates and the theories associated with them are reconsidered in light of the new findings.

21 The Missing Mass Problem

Clusters of galaxies appear to be large-scale stable configurations, with individual galaxies held in place by gravitational attraction. By using experimentally determined velocities of the galaxies, it is possible to calculate the mass necessary to keep the cluster stable. If this calculation is carried out for the Virgo cluster and the necessary mass is compared to the observed mass, it turns out that the mass needed to keep the cluster stable is fifty times the mass observed!

This is referred to as the *missing mass problem.* Because the mass is unseen, it is called *dark matter.* Various proposals have been made for candidates to carry the missing mass, but the candidates have been difficult to find. According to some researchers, such missing matter might make up more than 90 percent of the mass of the universe.

22 | Black Holes, White Holes, Worm Holes

Three unusual states of matter have been predicted to correspond to matter of infinite density: *black holes*—matter of infinite density into which other matter would be attracted; *white holes*—an infinite source from which mass would continually pour forth; and *worm holes*—a combination of the other two.

Because black holes are so dense, the speed necessary to escape from them would have to be greater than what appears to be the universal speed limit, the speed of light. Thus, they are called *black holes* because they could give off no light. Because the instrumentation for detecting celestial objects is keyed to analysis of the electromagnetic radiation they give off, black holes would seem impossible to detect.

However, there might be a solution to this problem. If black holes are formed by large stars at the end of their life cycle (when gravity wins the struggle and pulls everything in), it might be possible that, in a system in which two stars orbit one another (binary stars), one that becomes a black hole might pull gases from its companion. Theory predicts that such gases would be heated to very high temperatures and thus emit X rays before being engulfed. So, if a weak X-ray source was found near a normal star, it might be evidence of a nearby black hole. In 1970, detectors placed aboard satellites detected just such a phenomenon.

Whereas black holes have some observational support, white holes and worm holes remain purely theoretical possibilities.

23 Earthquake Prediction

The test of a hypothesis is whether it makes predictions that are borne out. Unfortunately, geologists do not yet have a clear enough understanding of earthquake phenomena to predict reliably and consistently where and when earthquakes will occur.

In 1975, Chinese researchers used *foreshocks* (an increasing tide of small quakes) to accurately predict the devastating Haicheng quake. Foreshocks were also noted before an earthquake in California in 1975. Unfortunately, many earthquakes do not have foreshocks, making such pattern detection an unreliable guide at best.

Changes in the shape of the ground's surface were noticed just before a major earthquake in California in 1966 and one in Japan in 1944. Shape changes, however, are unreliable because rainfall, drying, and natural slumping continually change the shape of the landscape.

A truly effective scheme of practical earthquake prediction will have to be based on a combination of clues, so that decisions can be as firmly based as possible before warnings to evacuate are given.

24 Chaos Theory, Weather Prediction, and the Butterfly Effect

haos theory provides a way of seeing order and pattern where formerly only the random, erratic, and unpredictable—the chaotic—had been observed. It tries to explain how tiny differences in input can quickly become overwhelming differences in output, a phenomenon given the name *Sensitive Dependence on Initial Conditions.*

Chaos theory helps explain many phenomena, for example, the lack of success in forecasting weather more than a few days in advance. With the advent of widespread reporting stations, rapid data transmission, and computerized recording and forecasting, many people thought weather forecasts would be better than ever—they are not.

The large-scale computerized simulations that model weather are very sensitive to small variations in initial conditions. That means that in principle, a tiny event on one side of the world can dramatically influence large-scale weather patterns on the other side of the world a week or so later: A change in direction of a butterfly's flight in China, for example, can make a small change in the air pressure there, which becomes magnified and produces a major weather maker in the eastern United States the next week. Hence, the name for this effect: *The Butterfly Effect.*

25 Geological Similarities between Earth and Other Planets

Spacecraft missions to the planets have provided a flood of data to help in understanding the nature of these celestial bodies. Data from space probes have shown that concentric layers dominate the internal structure of all planets. The inner, or terrestrial, planets—Mercury, Venus, Earth, and Mars—are composed mostly of rocky materials surrounding metallic cores. The outer planets—Jupiter, Saturn, Uranus, and Neptune—lack solid surfaces and consist mostly of hydrogen, helium, and ices of water, methane, and ammonia. Pluto, the outermost planet (thus far), has more in common with the icy moons of the outer solar system than with the other outer planets. It is probably covered by frozen nitrogen and methane and probably has rock and ice in its interior.

Geologic processes similar to those on Earth occur on other planets. Evidence of past volcanic activity has been found on Mars and Venus. A magnetic field on Mercury hints at the presence of an iron-rich interior that might still be molten. Another possibility for Mercury is a solid core with a residual or inherited field from earlier times when a molten core permanently magnetized itself as it cooled.

26 Formation of Earth's Moon: The Giant Impact Theory

Various theories about the origin of Earth's moon have been proposed. Once astronauts gained firsthand information by landing on the moon and bringing back samples, several theories that were inconsistent with the new data were discarded, and a new one was proposed, the *Giant Impact Theory:* At about the time of Earth's formation, a Mars-sized celectial body collided with Earth. As a result of the violence of the collision, chunks of both the impactor and Earth's mantle were vaporized. Some of the vaporized chunks fell back to Earth, but others had enough energy to orbit Earth, where gravity worked on them, causing them to coalesce and form the moon.

This theory helps explain one of the previously puzzling aspects of lunar rocks, namely, their lack of volatile elements. The high-energy impact could have heated these rocks to the point where volatile elements boiled off. Computer simulations of this event have calculated the mass and likely trajectory of the impactor and yielded results consistent with the composition and ages of lunar materials.

27 | The Lock-and-Key Theory of Enzymes

Enzymes are vital parts of living cells. An average cell may contain some 3,000 different enzymes. They act in cells as catalysts (substances that cause a reaction to proceed faster without being permanently consumed by the reaction). Each enzyme is able to catalyze a specific reaction in which a particular molecule is converted into appropriate products. Enzymes can increase the rate of biochemical reactions by factors ranging from 10^6 (1,000,000) to 10^{12} (1,000,000,000,000)!

According to the lock-and-key theory for enzymatic catalysis, a molecule fits onto a specific site on the enzyme that catalyzes it in much the same way that a key fits into a particular lock: It is structurally compatible with that site.

It is generally agreed that this analogy is an oversimplification. Portions of the enzyme molecule other than the part that fits may also be involved in the catalytic process.

28 A Biology-Geology Linkage

The Earth's magnetic field deflects many of the charged particles coming from the sun and other sources. If undeflected, such energetic particles could cause mutations in DNA molecules, contributing to the creation of diversity among life forms.

During magnetic field reversals, which occur at irregular intervals an average of 600,000 years apart, the field is absent for a few thousand years. A fascinating hypothesis is that during this period, the additional charged-particle flux causes extremely rapid mutation rates. Once the magnetic field is back "on" and north and south poles are reestablished, but in reverse order, the particles are deflected again, and mutation rates return to normal.

Thus, according to this hypothesis, the development of complexity in organisms occurs in spurts, about 600,000 years apart. Because of the difficulty in obtaining hard evidence, this hypothesis remains speculative.

29 The Order in Which Life Developed

The logical order in which life developed is hypothesized to include the following stages:

1. Simple molecules underwent spontaneous, random chemical reactions. After about a half billion years, complex nucleic acid molecules were produced.
2. Molecules that could replicate (most likely, nucleic acid molecules), along with enzymes and nutrient molecules surrounded by a membrane formed cells.
3. Cells learned how to reproduce by copying DNA, which contains complete instructions for building a next generation of cells. During the reproduction process, mutations occurred. Changed DNA produced cells that differed from the original cells.
4. The variety of cells generated attempted to survive, reproduce, and create a next generation of cells in their likeness. Those better able to survive than others became more numerous in the population.

Historically, the fourth stage was the first to be understood. An understanding of the earlier stages came later, after atoms and molecules were better understood.

30 | Viruses: Dead or Alive?

An ongoing debate among biologists is whether viruses are living or dead, animate or inanimate. Some viruses are shaped very much like inanimate mineral crystals; others resemble living organisms, such as the euglena. Like inanimate material, the virus has no means of locomotion, possesses no source of energy, and cannot grow. On the other hand, viruses contain DNA or RNA and, like living matter, can reproduce (but not until they have commandeered a cell).

If a virus is alive, it is the smallest and simplest object that can be said to be alive. It acts as if it's alive when, within just an hour, an army of viruses invade living cells and leaves them broken husks of what they had been. This process is called a disease when the virus infects human cells, or those of plants or animals.

At the least, viruses are links between life and nonlife, bridges between living and nonliving matter. They might even resemble some of the first living organisms.

31 The Human Genome Project

Organisms inherit their traits by transmission of discrete units of information known as *genes.* The complete complement of an organism's genes is called its *genome.* A major project in biology is the attempt to determine the precise specification of the chromosomal locations and molecular composition of the thousands of genes comprising the human genome.

The human genome in a fertilized human egg constitutes the complete set of instructions for development. It determines the timing and details of the formation of the heart, the central nervous system, the immune system, and every other organ and tissue required for life. Genes at particular locations can have a pronounced effect on predisposition and resistance to particular diseases. Because maladies such as cystic fibrosis and Huntington's chorea are encoded in the genome by a defect in a single gene, mapping the human genome can lead to development of methods for early diagnosis and treatment of these and other diseases.

32 Potentially Dangerous Knowledge

Many people believe that some scientific ideas are potentially harmful to the entire human endeavor and, therefore, should not be pursued. They fear such ideas might fall into the hands of someone so unscrupulous that he or she would use the ideas to destroy all humankind.

This argument, phrased in many different ways, is sometimes used to suggest which avenues of scientific research should not be undertaken. In the main, the argument has merit, for humans certainly have the capacity to act irrationally, destroying whatever is in their path, including each other. The difficulty lies in using the argument in regard to a particular topic because potential uses of an area of basic understanding are far from clear in the beginning stages.

How could Rutherford, or anyone else for that matter, have known that application of knowledge about the atomic nucleus would lead to the development of the atomic bomb? How could he have known that hundreds of thousands of people would be killed and billions would be held hostage by the threatened use of such weapons?

33 Recombinant Engineering: A Pandora's Box?

Until the advent of human beings, the changes in DNA molecules that generated variety in the biosphere probably were almost totally random. As a result, evolutionary processes occurred slowly and were compatible with the environment. Recently, scientists have developed ways to remove some of the randomness of evolution. They have perfected techniques that enable them to make deliberate changes in DNA molecules, and they are now able to custom-build organisms.

One technique, *recombinant engineering,* involves removing portions of DNA collections and recombining them with other DNAs to produce an altered DNA collection. Proponents of recombinant engineering argue that scientists are on the verge of learning fascinating new details of the working of life; that scientific inquiry must proceed freely and openly; and that many practical benefits such as disease-resistant plants, might ensue. Opponents argue that scientists might be opening a Pandora's box by creating and accidentally releasing potentially harmful organisms that have no natural enemies to keep them in check.

34 Cloning: Carbon Copies

A *clone* is a lineage of genetically identical individuals. Single cells are routinely cloned in laboratories simply by isolating them in a suitable culture medium and allowing their descendants to form colonies of cells.

Clones can also be created by removing the genetic content of a cell taken from a donor and implanting this material into an egg cell whose nucleus has been removed. The new egg contains all the genetic information that gave rise to the donor. In the early 1960s, African clawed frogs were cloned by this technique. Rabbit embryos have been produced by cloning. Recently, a mouse clone became the first fully mature mammalian clone.

Can and will cloning of a human being follow? Should research that might make possible carbon-copy human beings be continued? Where, if anywhere, should the line be drawn?

35 | Extraterrestrial Life

According to astronomers, the development of the solar system is not necessarily unique. It follows that there might be other planets that house intelligent civilizations. To estimate the possible number of other human civilizations requires assessing a variety of factors that contribute to their likelihood. An equation used to make this estimate is the *Drake Equation.*

If use of this equation is restricted to just this galaxy, the Milky Way, a starting point is the number of stars formed per year. Because there are 200 billion stars in the Milky Way and this galaxy's lifetime is about 10 billion years, the average is about 20 stars per year. Other factors include the fraction of stars that provide conditions suitable for life to develop on planets, the fraction of such stars with planets, the fraction of planets on which life actually develops, the fraction of life that is intelligent, the fraction of intelligent life that is communicative, and the lifetime of communicative civilizations.

Depending on the values given each of the estimates, numbers from one to several hundred million possible civilizations in the Milky Way have been calculated, with an average of around one million. In the hope of detecting communications from such civilizations, the electromagnetic spectrum reaching Earth is being scanned at various frequencies to look for signs of life. Stay tuned.

36 Global Warming: Radiative Equilibrium

The Earth's surface is warmed by radiation received from the sun. It is cooled as it emits radiation into space. When the rates at which radiation is received and emitted are equal, a state of *radiative equilibrium* exists. Under this condition, the average temperature at the Earth's surface remains constant. This temperature supports the development of life as it is known on Earth.

New factors have been introduced, especially in the twentieth century, that increase the amount of heat at the Earth's surface and that can alter the Earth's radiative equilibrium: Power plants dump vast amounts of residual heat into the environment. Overpopulation and urbanization result in so much human activity in cities that they are often 4 or 5°C warmer than surrounding areas. In the atmosphere, CO_2 gases from fossil-fuel combustion act to reflect back the radiation given off by Earth, much as the glass in a greenhouse holds in heat energy.

Fortunately, because of the Earth's huge mass, temperature changes occur slowly. Nevertheless, it is in the best interest of life on Earth to monitor the situation as closely as possible.

37 | Geothermal Energy

The Earth's internal heat is a huge potential source of energy. This geothermal energy is released naturally in geysers and volcanoes. Significant amounts of geothermal energy have long been used in Italy, New Zealand, and Iceland. A commercial geothermal plant at the Geysers in Sonoma County, California, is contributing to the energy resources of that state.

There are other schemes for harnessing the Earth's internal heat. One would be a power plant in which cold water passes through a vertically oriented crack (produced by humanly engineered hydraulic fracturing) to a region 5 kilometers below the surface of the Earth. There, it is heated to 300°C by dry hot rock before returning to the power plant.

Expansion of the use of geothermal energy presents a number of problems. One of these is disposal of the waste water produced because the water picks up and dissolves many salts along the way, salts that can contaminate ground water and poison fish and other aquatic life.

38 Disposal of Unwanted By-Products

By-products of processes such as geothermal energy production are considered wastes if a suitable use for them cannot be found. Some waste materials pose serious problems because they threaten human health or the environment when managed improperly.

It is difficult to avoid creation of hazardous wastes because they are by-products of the production of such commonly used materials as textiles, leather, metals, oil, and gasoline. These wastes can react spontaneously with each other, react vigorously with water or air, contain or release toxic substances, and corrode container materials.

The problem of disposal of radioactive wastes is especially difficult because many fission products are dangerous radioactive isotopes with long half-lives. Such wastes must often be isolated from the environment for thousands of years. Suggestions for storage or disposal include burial underground, burial beneath the ocean floor, and storage in deep geological formations.

39 Genesis of the Ozone Layer: Chemical Equilibrium

After the evolution of photosynthesis, large amounts of free oxygen in the form of O_2 molecules were generated. These molecules reached the upper atmosphere, where they were decomposed into oxygen atoms (O) by radiation from the sun:

$$O_2 \rightarrow O + O$$

Collision of the oxygen atoms and O_2 molecules produced ozone (O_3):

$$O_2 + O \rightarrow O_3$$

The ozone molecule does not last long. It can absorb solar radiation, which results in its decomposition into O_2 and O:

$$O_3 \rightarrow O_2 + O$$

When the rate at which ozone is formed is equal to the rate at which it decomposes, a state of chemical equilibrium exists in which the concentration of ozone in the atmosphere is constant. This equilibrium is analogous to radiative equilibrium. (Refer back to Idea Folder 36 for a discussion of radiative equilibrium.)

40 | Smaller and Faster Computers: Biochips, Atomchips and Spinchips

The invention of modern computers required devices that could code information as a series of yes-or-no bits, for example, 1s-or-0s or on-or-off switches. The first modern computer used *vacuum tubes* (evacuated electron tubes that can act as a kind of valve for electrical flow). The yes-or-no bits corresponded to the vacuum tubes being on or off. Beginning in 1947, *transistors* (devices containing *semiconductors,* crystalline substances able to conduct electricity better than insulators but not as well as good conductors) replaced the relatively large and slow vacuum tubes. Since then, the development of even smaller devices, called *microchips* (silicon-chip microprocessors) has made possible yet smaller and faster computers.

Further size reduction, along with increased energy efficiency and speed, might result from the development of *biochips* (organic molecules manufactured by bacteria designed by genetic engineering). The yes-or-no bits in biochips could correspond to the presence or absence of atoms at a particular site in a collection of molecules. Even further size reduction and increased speed could be achieved in *atomchips* by using the presence or absence of individual atoms at a particular location in a collection of atoms. Ultimate size reduction and speed increase might be possible by taking advantage of the fact that electrons in a normal electric current spin in a random mix of two quantum states: up and down. Using magnets, scientists have been able to create these two states and, thus, the on-or-off switches required for *spinchips.*

Additional Reading

After reading this overview of science, you might wish to read some of the following books.

The Method of Science

Beardsley, M. C. *Thinking Straight*. 2nd ed. Englewood Cliffs, NJ: Prentice-Hall, 1965.

Carey, S. S. *A Beginner's Guide to Scientific Method*. Belmont, CA: Wadsworth, 1994.

Casti, J. L. *Five Golden Rules: Great Theories of 20th Century Mathematics and Why They Matter*. New York: John Wiley & Sons, 1995.

Gingerich, O. *The Nature of Scientific Discovery*. Washington, DC: Smithsonian Institution Press, 1975.

Holton, G. *Thematic Origins of Scientific Thought: Kepler to Einstein*. Cambridge, MA: Harvard University Press, 1988.

Roberts, R. M. *Serendipity: Accidental Discoveries in Science*. New York: John Wiley & Sons, 1989.

Physics' Model of the Atom

Ehrlich, R. *The Cosmological Milk Shake: A Semi-serious Look at the Size of Things*. New Brunswick, NJ: Rutgers University Press, 1994.

Lederman, L. *The God Particle: If the Universe Is the Answer, What Is the Question?* New York: Houghton Mifflin, 1993.

Spielberg, N., and Anderson, B. D. *Seven Ideas That Shook the Universe.* 2nd ed. New York: John Wiley & Sons, 1995.

Trefil, J. *From Atoms to Quarks.* New York: Anchor Books, 1993.

Weinberg, S. *Dreams of a Final Theory.* New York: Pantheon Books, 1992.

Chemistry's Periodic Law

Asimov, I. *Asimov on Chemistry.* Garden City, NY: Anchor Books, 1975.

Hill, J. W. *Chemistry for Changing Times.* 6th ed. New York: Macmillan, 1992.

Knight, D. M. *Ideas in Chemistry.* New Brunswick, NJ: Rutgers University Press, 1992.

Snyder, C. *The Extraordinary Chemistry of Ordinary Things.* New York: John Wiley & Sons, 1992.

Astronomy's Big Bang Theory

Goldsmith, D. *Supernova! The Exploding Star of 1987.* New York: St. Martin's Press, 1989.

Hawking, S. W. *A Brief History of Time: From the Big Bang to Black Holes.* New York: Bantam Books, 1988.

Moché, D. L. *Astronomy, A Self-Teaching Guide.* 4th ed. New York: John Wiley & Sons, 1993.

Silk, J. *The Big Bang.* New York: W. H. Freeman, 1989.

Geology's Plate Tectonics Model

Cvancara, A. *A Field Manual for the Amateur Geologist.* New York: John Wiley & Sons, 1995.

Parker, R. *Inscrutable Earth.* New York: Scribner, 1984.

Weiner, J. *Planet Earth.* New York: Bantam Books, 1986.

Wyllie, P. J. *The Way the Earth Works: An Introduction to the New Global Geology and Its Revolutionary Development.* New York: John Wiley & Sons, 1976.

Biology's Theory of Evolution

Deamer, D. W., and Fleischaker, G. R., eds. *Origins of Life: The Central Concepts.* Boston: James and Bartlett, 1994.

de Duve, C. *Vital Dust: Life as a Cosmic Imperative.* New York: Basic Books, 1995.

Eldredge, N. *Reinventing Darwin: The Great Debate at the High Table of Evolutionary Theory.* New York: John Wiley & Sons, 1995.

Garber, S. D. *Biology, A Self-Teaching Guide.* New York: John Wiley & Sons, 1989.

Watson, J. D. *The Double Helix.* New York: Athaneum, 1985.

Wilson, E. O. *The Diversity of Life.* New York: Norton, 1992.

Benefit/Risk Analysis

Landau, L. *Running Risks.* New York: John Wiley & Sons, 1994.

Potter, V. R. *Bioethics: Bridge to the Future.* Englewood Cliffs, NJ: Prentice-Hall, 1971.

Wakeford, T., and Walters, M. *Science for the Earth: Can Science Make the World a Better Place?* New York: John Wiley & Sons, 1995.

Wheeler, D., and Janis, I. L. *A Practical Guide for Making Decisions.* New York: The Free Press, 1980.

Energy Resources

Aubrecht, G. J. *Energy.* 2nd ed. New York: Prentice-Hall, 1995.

Fowler, J. M. *Energy and the Environment.* 2nd ed. New York: McGraw-Hill, 1984.

Meador, R. *Future Energy Alternatives: Long Range Energy Prospects for America and the World.* Ann Arbor, MI: Ann Arbor Science, 1978.

Schneider, S. *Global Warming: Are We Entering the Greenhouse Century?* San Francisco: Sierra Club Books, 1989.

Chlorofluorocarbon Spray-Can Propellants

Benedict, R. *Ozone Diplomacy: New Directions in Safeguarding the Planet.* Cambridge, MA: Harvard University Press, 1991.

Cagin, S., and Dray, P. *Between Earth and Sky: How CFCs Changed Our World and Endangered the Ozone Layer.* New York: Pantheon Books, 1993.

Dotto, L., and Schiff, H. *The Ozone War.* New York: Doubleday, 1978.

Setterberg, F., and Shavelson, L. *Toxic Nation: The Fight to Save Our Communities from Chemical Contamination.* New York: John Wiley & Sons, 1993.

Computerized Credit and Banking Information

Branscomb, A. W. *Who Owns Information?: From Privacy to Public Access.* New York: BasicBooks, 1994.

Cooper, J. A. *Computer and Communications Security: Strategies for the 1990s.* New York: McGraw-Hill, 1989.

Fites, P. E. *Control and Security of Computer Information Systems.* Rockville, MD: Computer Science Press, 1989.

Stoll, C. *Silicon Snake Oil: Second Thoughts on the Information Highway.* New York: Doubleday, 1995.

Index

A

abstractions, 108–116
aether, 33
Africa, continental drift,
    70–72, 71f
air, 32–33
alchemy, 44
algae cytoplasm and nucleus ex-
    periment, 85–87, 86f, 88f
aluminum, 37–38
anaximenes, 32
animal cells, 84f, 84–85
antimatter, vs. matter, 153
Aristotle, 13–16, 33, 82–84
asexual reproduction, 97f, 97–99,
    98f, 100f
asthenosphere, 73
astronomy, 47–64
    age of the universe, 48, 163
    black holes, white holes, and
        worm holes, 62, 165
    continued expansion theory,
        59–61, 60f
    cosmic linkages, 59
    defined, 12
    extraterrestrial life, 178
    future of universe, 59–61
    limitations of science, 62–64
    missing mass problem, 164
    models of the universe, 10–11

big bang theory, 49–55, 54f,
    56f, 111
    geocentric, 48
    heliocentric, 48–49
    supernovas, 55–57, 57f
nebular hypothesis, 58, 81
observations, 47–48
    instruments for, 162
    in perspective, 161
oscillating universe theory,
    59–61, 60f
resources on, 186
similarities between
    planets, 168
atmosphere, 162. *See also* ozone
    origin of life and, 91–95
the atom, 13–29
    in Big Bang theory, 53–55, 54f
    chemical properties, 32
    Einstein's theories of special and
        general relativity, 158
    electricity and magnetism, 156
    electromagnetic radiation inter-
        action with matter, 148
    forces in nature, 155
    fusing elements, 43–44
    Heisenberg's uncertainty princi-
        ple, 24–25, 26f, 152
    matter, 31
    matter vs. antimatter, 153

the atom (*cont.*)
  models of
    Aristotle vs. Democritus
      model of matter, 13–16, 14f,
      18f
    Bohr's, 20–23, 21f, 23f, 26f,
      111–112, 113–114
    Dalton's, 16
    evolution of, 28f
    Quantum Mechanical Model,
      23–24
    Rutherford's Solar System
      Model, 18–20, 20f, 23f
    a scaled-up model, 150
    Thomson's Plum Pudding
      Model, 17–18, 18f, 20f, 21f
  Newton's laws of motion and
    gravitation, 157
  quarks, 26–27, 27f
  resources on, 185–186
  scanning tunneling microscopy,
    154
  Schrödinger's cat, 151
  spherical shape, 18
  studying, 10
  wave vs. particle model of light,
    149
atomchips, 183–184
atomic masses
  Dalton's theories, 16
  discovery of, 35
  in periodic table, 35–40
  triads, 35–36
atomic number
  fusing elements, 43–44
  notation for, 43–44
  in periodic law, 40, 41f
authority in science, 14–16, 28–29

B
bacteria
  capsule experiment, 87–89
  penicillin-resistant, 104–105
balloon example of universe, 50,
  52
banking information, 134–137, 188
benefit/risk analysis, 124–138

chlorofluorocarbons, 130–134
computer technology, 134–137,
  183–184
decisions about resources,
  125–130
geothermal energy, 180
global warming, 179
model of, 124, 124f
ozone layer, 182
resources on, 187
waste disposal, 181
Bernard, Claude, 31
beryllium, 55
Big Bang theory
  age of the universe, 163
  balloon analogy, 50, 52
  black holes, white holes, and
    worm holes in, 62
  cosmic linkages, 59
  expansion of universe, 50–51
  future of universe and, 59–61,
    60f
  helium and background radia-
    tion, 52–53
  Hubble's observations, 49–50
  hypothesis, 111
  limitations of, 62–64
  nebular hypothesis, 58, 81
  primeval fireball explosion,
    51–52
  resources on, 186
  stars in element creation, 53–55,
    54f, 56f
  supernovas in, 55–56, 57f
Big Crunch theory, 59–61, 60f
biochips, 183
biology, 81–106
  cell structure and function, 84f,
    84–85
    nucleus and cytoplasm, 85–87,
      86f, 88f
  cloning, 177
  defined, 12, 81–82
DNA
  discovery of, 87–89
  function, 89–90
enzyme theory, 170

ethical issues, 175
evolutionary theory
  atmosphere in, 94–95
  DDT-resistant mosquitos,
    104–105
  genetic material, 96–100, 97f,
    98f, 100f
  limitations of, 105
  mutations and magnetic field,
    171
  mutations and natural selec-
    tion, 95–96, 101–104, 102f,
    103f
  order of development in, 172
  origin of life, 91f, 91–93, 92f, 94f
  penicillin-resistant bacteria, 104
  spontaneous generation and,
    105, 106f
  tree of life, 103f, 104
extraterrestrial life, 178
Human Genome Project, 174
molecular basis of life, 90–91
recombinant engineering, 176
resources on, 187
spontaneous generation of complex organisms, 82–84
viruses, 173
black boxes
  coffee machine example, 7–8
  defined, 6
  in scientific method, 6–8
black holes, 62, 165
Bohr's model of the atom, 20–23,
    28f, 111–112, 113–114
  vs. Quantum Mechanical Model,
    26f
  vs. Rutherford's Solar System
    Model, 23f
Bolos of Mendes, 33
boron, 37–38
bromine, 39
Butterfly Effect, 167

C
calcium, 38, 39
California, 76, 166
cancer, 131–132

carbon, 91
  fusing with hydrogen, 43–44
  organic chemistry, 160
Carlyle, Thomas, 47
cathode rays, 17
"ceci n'est pas une pipe" (Magritte),
  109
cell
  atmospheric evolution, 94–95
  cytoplasm and nucleus algae ex-
    periment, 85–87, 86f, 88f
  differentiation, 99
  DNA
    bacteria experiment, 87–89
    function, 89–90
  in evolutionary theory, 172
  molecular basis of, 90–91
  mutations, 101
  origin of life, 91f, 91–93, 92f
  reproduction, 97f, 97–100, 98f,
    100f
  requirements for existence, 90
  structure and function, 84f,
    84–89, 90f
cell membrane, 84
chaos theory, 167
charge, of electrons, 17–18
chemical properties, in periodic
  table, 34–40
chemical reactions, in origin of
  life, 91–93, 94f
chemistry, 31–46
  alchemy, 33–34
  defined, 12, 32
  fusion of elements, 43–44
  Greek and Egyptian view of the
    elements, 32–33
  inductive reasoning, 110
  isotopes, 44
  matter, 31
  naming new elements, 44–46
  organic vs. inorganic, 160
  origin of word, 33
  the periodic table, 34–43
    atomic mass and chemical
      properties in, 34–39, 36f,
      38f, 39f, 40f

chemistry (*cont.*)
    atomic numbers in, 40, 41f
    Mendeleev's, 36f
    modern version, 40–41, 42f
    in predicting new elements, 43
    scandium in, 39f
    tellurium and iodine in, 40f
    titanium in, 38f
  radioisotopes, 44, 159
  resources on, 186
chlorine, 39, 110
chlorofluorocarbons, 130–134, 188
chromosomes, 84. *See also* DNA
cloning, 176
coffee machine example, 7–8
Coma (Cook), 5–6
computers
  benefit/risk analysis of technol-
    ogy, 134–137, 183–184, 188
  in weather prediction, 167
Constant Composition, Law of, 16
continental drift, 70–72, 71f, 75f,
    75–76
continued expansion theory,
    59–61, 60f
Cook, Robin, 5–6
Copernican theory, 48–49
core of Earth, 73
cosmic background radiation,
    52–53
credit information, 134–137, 188
crust of Earth, 72
cytoplasm, 84, 85–87

D

Dalton's model of the atom, 16
dark matter, 62, 164
Darwin, Charles, 95–96
DDT-resistant mosquitos, 104–105
deabstraction, 116
deBroglie, Louis, 149
deductive reasoning, 114–115
Democritus's model of the atom,
    13–16, 14f, 28f
  vs. Dalton's model, 16
  vs. Thomson's Plum Pudding
    Model, 17, 18f

density of rocks, 67–68, 74
deoxyribonucleic acid. *See* DNA
differentiation of cells, 99
DNA (deoxyribonucleic acid)
  change in over time, 96–97
  discovery of, 87–89
  function of, 89–90
  in meiosis, 99–100, 100f
  in mitosis, 97f, 97–99, 98f
  mutations and natural selection,
    101–105, 171, 172
  personal self-consciousness and,
    121
  in primitive molecules, 92, 172
  recombinant engineering, 176
  tree of life, 103f, 104
Dobereiner, Johann, 35
Drake Equation, 178
dubnium, 44–46

E

Earth. *See also* geology
  atmosphere, 91–95
  continental drift, 70–72, 71f, 75f
  density of rocks, 67–68
  earthquakes and volcanoes, 69,
    69f
  gravitational force of, 59–60
  magnetic field, 68–69, 78f, 79f,
    171
  models of
    geocentric, 48–49
    heliocentric, 48
    history of, 65–67
    Plate Tectonics Model, 72–79,
      73f
  nebular hypothesis, 81–82
  seismic waves, 69–70, 71f
earthquakes, 74, 76, 166
  geographic zones, 69, 69f, 74
economic issues. *See* benefit/risk
    analysis
Egyptians, experimentation, 33
Einstein's theories of relativity,
    158
electric charge, of electrons, 17–18
electricity, magnetism and, 155

electromagnetic force, 148, 155
electronic fund transfer, 135
electron microscopes, limitations, 10
electrons, 152
  antiparticles, 153
  in Bohr's model of the atom, 22, 111–112, 113–114
  in Quantum Mechanical Model, 24
  Thomson's model of, 17–18
electroweak force, 155
elements
  atomic masses, 34–35
  in Big Bang theory, 53–55, 54f, 56f
  chemical properties of, 32
  defined, 32
  fusing, 43–44
  Greek and Egyptian view of, 32–33
  isotopes, 44
  Law of Constant Composition, 16
  naming new, 44–46
  triads, 35–36
  universal, 32–33
Empedocles, 32–33
energy, of atoms, 111–112, 113–114
energy resources
  benefit/risk analysis, 125–130, 180
  resources on, 187–188
environmental issues, benefit/risk analysis
  chlorofluorocarbons, 130–134
  energy resources, 125–130
  geothermal energy, 180
  global warming, 179
  ozone layer, 182
  waste disposal, 181
enzymes
  function, 89–90
  lock-and-key theory of, 170
ethical issues
  benefit/risk analysis, 124–138
    chlorofluorocarbons, 130–134

computer technology, 134–137, 183–184
  decisions about resources, 125–130
  geothermal energy, 180
  global warming, 179
  model of, 124, 124f
  ozone layer, 182
  waste disposal, 181
  origin of ethical codes, 122–123
  in research, 175, 176, 177
  scientific method and, 123
evolutionary theory
  atmosphere in, 94–95
  DDT-resistant mosquitos, 104–105
  genetic material, 96–100, 97f, 98f, 100f
  humans
    ethical codes, 122–124
    personal self-consciousness, 120f, 120–121
    social self-consciousness, 121–122, 122f
  information-transmitting structures, 120f
  limitations of, 105
  mutations and magnetic field, 171
  mutations and natural selection, 95–96, 101–104, 102f, 103f
  Oparin's hypothesis, 93
  order of development in, 172
  origin of life, 91f, 91–93, 92f, 94f
  penicillin-resistant bacteria, 104
  resources on, 187
  spontaneous generation and, 105, 106f
  tree of life, 103f, 104
experiments
  as authority in science, 15–16
  vs. observation, 107–108
  performed by Egyptians, 33
  from prediction to, 115–116
  in scientific method, 2, 116–117, 118f
extraterrestrial life, 146, 178

F
fire, 32–33
fluorine, 39
forces of nature, 155
foreshocks, 166
fossil fuels, 125–130
fusion, in Big Bang theory, 54–55,
   56f

G
galaxies
   expanding universe, 50
   gravitational attraction, 164
   Milky Way, 178
Galileo, 49
gas clouds, in Big Bang theory,
   53–55, 54f
Geiger counter, 159
genes, 96. *See also* DNA
genetics. *See also* DNA
   cloning, 177
   Human Genome Project, 174
   recombinant engineering, 176
geocentric model of the universe,
   48–49
geology, 65–80
   continental drift, 70–72, 71f, 75f
   defined, 12
   density of rocks, 67–68
   Earth and other planets, 168
   earthquakes and volcanoes, 69,
      69f, 166
   magnetic field, 68–69, 78f, 79f, 171
   models of the Earth
      geocentric, 48–59
      heliocentric, 48
      history of, 65–67
      Plate Tectonics Model, 72–79,
         73f
   the moon's formation, 169
   resources on, 186–187
   sea-floor spreading, 77f
   seismic waves, 69–70, 71f
   weather prediction, 167
geosynchronous satellites, 157
geothermal energy, 180
gestalt, 140–141

Giant Impact Theory, 169
Gide, André, 119
global warming, 179
gold
   alchemy, 33–34
   platinum isotope decay, 44
Goodyear, Charles, 145
Grand Unified Theory (GUT), 155
gravitation, 155
   in Big Bang theory, 54
   of Earth, 59–60
   end of universe and, 60–61
   missing mass problem, 164
   Newton's law of, 157
   universal, 157
   of universe, 60
Greeks
   model of matter, 13–16, 14f, 18f
   universal elements, 32–33

H
Haicheng earthquake, 166
hazardous wastes, 181
Heisenberg's uncertainty principle, 24–25, 152
heliocentric model of the universe, 48–49
helium, in Big Bang theory, 52–53,
   54f, 54–55
Heraclitus, 32
Himalayas, 76
Hubble, Edwin, 50
Hubble space telescope, 162, 163
Human Genome Project, 174
humans
   ethical codes, 122–124
   meiosis and mitosis, 97–100
   personal self-consciousness,
      120f, 120–121
   social self-consciousness,
      121–122f
hydrogen
   atoms, 22
   in cells, 91
   fusing with carbon, 43–44
   nuclear fusion, 54–55
   in periodic table, 36

hypothesis
  in astronomy, 11
  defined, 2
  of Greek philosophers, 14–15
  vs. laws, theories, and models,
    113
  models and black boxes and, 6–8
  modifying, 116–117, 118f
  from observation to, 108–111
  Occam's Razor, 9, 146
  to prediction, 113–115
  representing reality, 111–112
  testing and revising, 2–3, 4

I
inductive reasoning, 110
information
  benefit/risk analysis, 134–137,
    188
  as resource, 125–126
information-transmitting struc-
    tures, 120f
International Union of Pure and
    Applied Chemistry (IUPAC),
    44–46
iodine, 39, 40f
isotopes
  creating, 43–44
  nuclear fusion in, 54–55
  platinum, 44
  radioisotopes, 43–44, 159
IUPAC (International Union of
    Pure and Applied Chem-
    istry), 44–46

J
Jansky, Karl, 162
Jupiter, 168

K
Koestler, Arthur, 81
kurchatovium, 44–46

L
laws
  defined, 3
  vs. hypotheses and theories, 113

leptons, 27
life. *See* evolutionary theory
light. *See* radiation
lithium, 36–37
lithosphere, 73
lock-and-key theory of enzymes,
    170
L-waves, 70

M
maggots, spontaneous generation,
    82–83
magnetism
  of Earth, 68–69, 74, 77–79, 78f,
    79f, 171
  electromagnetic force, 148, 155
  of Mercury, 168
Magritte, René, 109
mantle of Earth, 73
Many Worlds Interpretation, of
    Schrödinger's cat, 151
Mars, 168
mass
  in gravitational force, 60
  missing mass problem, 164
  of the universe, 60, 62
mathematics, 112, 114
matter
  vs. antimatter, 153
  Aristotle's vs. Democritus's
    model of, 13–14
  dark, 62, 164
  defined, 31
  electromagnetic radiation inter-
    action with, 148
  interaction with light, 148
  as resource, 125–126
meiosis, 99–100, 100f
Mendel, Gregor, 96
Mendeleev, Dimitri, 36–39
  version of periodic table, 36f
Mercury, 168
metric system, 147
microchips, 183
microscopes
  limitations, 10
  scanning tunneling, 154

microwaves, 53
Milky Way galaxy, 178
Miller, Stanley, 93, 94f
missing mass problem, 164
mitosis, 97f, 97–99, 98f, 100f
models. *See also specific models*
  coffee machine example, 7–8
  defined, 6
  in scientific method, 6–8
  vs. theories, 113
modern synthesis, 96
molecular biology, 96
molecules as basis of life, 90, 172.
  See also the atom
Molina-Rowland chlorofluorocarbon-ozone depletion model,
  132
moon, 169
morals. *See* ethical issues
mosquitos, DDT-resistant, 104–105
motion, Newton's law of, 157
mutations
  in evolutionary theory, 101–105
  magnetism in, 171
  random copy error, 101

N
natural selection
  in evolution, 101–104
natural selection, Darwin's theory
  of, 95–96
nature, forces of, 155
nebular hypothesis, 58, 81
neo-Darwinism, 96
neon lights, 20–21
Neptune, 168
neptunium, 44
neutrons, 24
  in Big Bang theory, 51–52, 54–55
  in isotopes, 44
neutron stars, 62
Newlands, John, 36
Newton's laws
  of motion and gravitation, 157
  Schrödinger's cat and, 151
nitrogen

  in atmosphere, 94–95
  in cells, 91
  fusing nuclei to create, 43–44
  isotopes, 44
nuclear forces in nature, 155
nuclear fusion, in Big Bang theory,
  54–55, 56f
nucleus
  atomic, 84
    in Big Bang theory, 51–52,
      54–55
    fusing elements, 43–44
    in isotopes, 44
  cell, algae experiment, 85–87,
    86f, 88f
nutrients, for cells, 90

O
observations
  in astronomy, 11
  vs. experimentation, 107–108
  to hypothesis, 108–111
  in scientific method, 2, 4, 5
Occam's Razor, 9, 146
On the Origin of Species (Darwin),
  95–96
Oparin, Alexander I., 93
operationalism, 144
orbits, in Bohr's model of the
  atom, 21–23
oscillating universe theory, 59–61,
  60f
oxygen
  in atmosphere, 94–95
  in cells, 91
  ozone layer and, 132, 182
  in periodic table, 37, 39
ozone
  chemical equilibrium, 182
  chlorofluorocarbon effects,
    130–134
  in early atmosphere, 95
ozonosphere, 131–132

P
Pangea, 75–76

particle model of light, 149
Pasteur, Louis, 145
penicillin-resistant bacteria,
    104–105
periodic law, 40
periodic table
    atomic mass and chemical prop-
        erties in, 34–39
    atomic numbers in, 40, 41f
    Mendeleev's version, 36f
    modern version, 40–41, 42f
    in predicting new elements, 43
    resources on, 186
    scandium in, 39f
    tellurium and iodine in, 40f
    titanium in, 38f
personal self-consciousness, 120f,
    120–121
Phillpotts, Eden, 13
philosophical presuppositions of
    science, 144
photosynthesis, 95
physics
    the atom, models of, 13–29,
        111–112, 113–114
    defined, 12
    Einstein's theories of special and
        general relativity, 158
    electricity and magnetism,
        156
    electromagnetic radiation inter-
        action with matter, 148
    forces in nature, 155
    matter vs. antimatter, 153
    Newton's laws of motion and
        gravitation, 157
    resources on, 185–186
    a scaled-up model of, 150
    scanning tunneling microscopy,
        154
    Schrödinger's cat, 151
    wave vs. particle model of light,
        149
pipe leak detection, 159
pitch of sound, 50
plant cells, 84–85

Plate Tectonics Model of the Earth,
    72–79, 73f
    asthenosphere, 73
    continental drift in, 75
    crust, 72
    earthquakes and volcanoes in,
        74, 76
    lithosphere, 73
    magnetic field in, 74
    mantle, 73
    outer and inner core, 73
    resources on, 186–187
    rock density in, 74
    seismic waves in, 75
platinum isotopes, 44
Pluto, 168
pneumonia, 87–89
pollution, 128
positrons, 153
prediction
    to experimentation, 115–116
    from hypothesis to, 113–115
    modifying, 116–117
    in scientific method, 2, 4, 118f
primeval fireball, 51
probems, in scientific method, 5
protons, 24
    in Big Bang theory, 51–52, 54–55
    fusing elements, 43–44
    in isotopes, 44
Ptolemaic theory, 48–49
P-waves, 70

Q
quantitative relationships, 111–112,
    113–114
Quantum Mechanical Model of
    the Atom, 23–24, 25, 28f
    vs. Bohr's model, 26f
    particle model of light and, 149
    Schrödinger's cat and, 151
quarks, 26–27, 27f

R
radiation
    in atmospheric evolution, 94–95

radiation (*cont.*)
  from atoms, 20–22
  in Big Bang theory, 52–53
  from black holes, 62
  Einstein's theories of relativity,
    158
  frequency and wavelength,
    148
  global warming, 179
  Heisenberg's uncertainty princi-
    ple, 152
  interaction with matter, 148
  in origin of life, 91–92
  ozone layer and, 131–132
  quantitative relationships,
    111–112, 113–114
  redshifting from other galaxies,
    50
  spectrum for observing the uni-
    verse, 162
  wave vs. particle model of, 149
radioactive wastes, 181
radioactivity, in investigations of
    the atom, 19
radio-frequency waves, 162
radioisotopes
  creating, 43–44
  as tracers, 159
random copy errors, 101–105
reasoning
  as authority, 28–29
  deductive, 114–115
  inductive, 110
recombinant engineering, 176
red giants, 56
Redi, Francesco, 83
redshifted light, 50
relativity, Einstein's theories of,
    158
representations, 108–116
reproduction, 97–100
resources, benefit/risk analysis,
    125–130
ribonucleic acid (RNA), 89–90, 92
risk analysis. *See* benefit/risk
    analysis

RNA (ribonucleic acid), 89–90, 92
rocks, density of, 67–68, 74
Rowland-Molina chlorofluorocar-
    bon-ozone depletion model,
    132
rubber vulcanization, 145
rutherfordium, 44–46
Rutherford's Solar System Model
    of the Atom, 18–20, 28f, 175
  vs. Thomson's Plum Pudding
    Model, 19, 20f, 21f

S
San Andreas Fault, 76
satellites, 157, 162
Saturn, 168
scandium, 38, 39f, 41
scanning tunneling microscopy,
    154
Schrödinger's cat, 151
scientific method, 2–12, 3f, 118f
  alternative views, 5
  applications, 5–6
  coffee machine example, 6–8
  domains of, 10–11
  elements of, 2–3
  ethical issues, 123, 175, 176, 177
    benefit/risk analysis,
      124–138
  experimentation, 107–108,
    115–116
  hypothesis
    vs. laws, theories, and models,
      113
    modifying, 116–117
    from observation to, 108–111
    to prediction, 113–115
    representing reality, 111–112
  limitations of, 62–63
  mathematics and, 112, 114
  metric system, 147
  models and black boxes, 6–8
  observation
    vs. experimentation, 107–108
    to hypothesis, 108–111
  Occam's Razor, 9, 146

philosophical presuppositions of, 144
prediction, 115–116
puppy example, 2–3
resources on, 185
serendipity and progress, 145
theories and laws, 3–4
sea-floor spreading, 77, 77f
seismic waves, 69–70, 71f, 75
  L-waves, 70, 71f
  P-waves, 61f, 70
  S-waves, 70, 71f
seismograph, 70
selenium, 39
self-consciousness, 120–122
semiconductors, 183
Sensitive Dependence on Initial Conditions, 167
serendipity, 145
sexual reproduction, 99–100, 100f
skin cancer, 131–132
social self-consciousness, 121–122, 122f
Sockman, Ralph W., 65
sodium, 36–37
solar system
  age of, 56
  geocentric model, 48
  heliocentric model, 48
  nebular hypothesis, 58, 81
  similarities between planets, 168
sound pitch, 50
South America, continental drift, 70–72, 71f
spinchips, 183–184
spontaneous generation
  of complex organisms, 82–84
  of first cell, 93, 105, 106f
spray-can propellants, 130–134, 188
stars, in Big Bang theory
  black holes, white holes, and worm holes, 62, 165
  cosmic linkages, 59
  element creation, 53–55, 54f, 56f
  neutron stars, 62
  supernovas, 55–56, 57f

strontium, 39
sulfur, 39
sun
  age of, 56
  in origin of life, 91–92
  in solar system models, 48–49
supernovas, 55–56, 57f
S-waves, 70
symbols, 108–116

T
telescopes, 49, 161, 162
tellurium, 39, 40f
temperature, in Big Bang theory, 51–52
Thales, 32
theories
  defined, 3
  vs. laws and models, 113
Thomson's Plum Pudding Model of the Atom, 17–18, 18f, 28f
  vs. Rutherford's Solar System Model, 19, 20f, 21f
titanium, 37–38, 38f, 40
tracers, radioisotopes, 159
traffic light example of inductive reasoning, 110–111
transistors, 183
transmutation of elements, 33–34, 44

U
UFOs, 146, 178
ultraviolet light, 94–95, 131–132
universal gravitation, 157
universe. See astronomy
unnilquadium, 44–46
uranium, 44, 154
Uranus, 168

V
vacuum tubes, 183
values. See ethical issues
Venus, 49, 168
viruses, 173

volcanoes, 74
   geographic zones, 69, 69f, 74
vulcanization of rubber, 145

W
waste disposal, 181
water, 32–33
wave model of light, 149
weather prediction, 167

white holes, 165
wood, 33
worm holes, 165

X
X-rays, from black holes, 165

Y
Yang, C. N., 112